AF304747

IMAGINING
THE
WORLD

IMAGINING THE WORLD

Daily Reflections for the Creation Season

JOHN MANN

DARTON · LONGMAN + TODD

INTELLIGENT · INSPIRATIONAL · INCLUSIVE
SPIRITUAL BOOKS

First published in 2026 by
Darton, Longman and Todd Ltd
Unit 1, The Exchange
6 Scarbrook Road
Croydon CR0 1UH
editorial@darton-longman-todd.co.uk

This product conforms to the requirements of the European Union's
General Product Safety Regulations (GPSR).
EU Authorised Representative for GPSR:
Easy Access System Europe –
Mustamäe tee 50, 10621 Tallinn, Estonia
gpsr.requests@easproject.com

ISBN: 978-1-917362-22-1

A catalogue record for this book is available from the British Library.

Printed and bound in Great Britain by Bell & Bain, Glasgow

To
Edward, Robyn and Patrick
May you live to see a new century
and a healed planet.

'She saw everything and everyone in a light of gold. She saw correspondences and analogies and echoes and resemblances, so that nothing existed without a thousand connections to the world, and I saw them with her. For her world was rich with meaning and alive with delight. Then little by little this way of seeing left her …'

Lyra's lost imagination – from The Rose Field, by Philip Pullman p.37

'This is what I know: without imagination you never see the truth about anything. Without imagination you think you see more truth, but in fact you see less.'

Words of 'a holy man from India' – from The Rose Field, p.56

Contents

Acknowledgements

SOME YEARS AGO on the death of the Reverend Ronald Dain, whose significant ministry in Nairobi had involved work as a theological educator and latterly as executive officer of the supporting organisation, CORAT (Christian Organizations Research and Advisory Trust of Africa) 1976-1979, I was given his collection of the works of Teilhard de Chardin, by Ronald's daughter Maggie. They lay unread on my shelves until, in retirement, I took them up and studied them one by one; they became one of the chief inspirations for this work. I have found the reflections by Père Teilhard of a century ago chiming in our own century, as assumed certainties that have existed all of my lifetime are being challenged, and years of adapting to a new situation have become our new expectation, bringing the Christian Church a fresh context as much as any other faith, or indeed, individual. A small paperback of Simone Weil's best-known work became my other go-to text, as she, with Père Teilhard, lived and wrote in a world of rapid change and great anxiety. So, I am grateful to Maggie Shaylor, and to her husband Charlie, who died, sadly, in early January 2026, and, with both of them, their parents too, as former parishioners and friends from the small village of Lasham in Hampshire.

The dedication of this book looks not to the distant past, but to the present and the future. My wife and I have three grandchildren, Edward and Patrick on our daughter's side, Robyn on our son's, with their respective and wonderful marriage partners. As we consider the environmental degradation and threat to the health and, indeed, existence of our planet, it is to the children and to future generations that my primary concern turns. The question of what condition we shall pass on the earth as we leave it has concentrated the minds and hearts of those older in years than the young, but not necessarily wiser or having longer sight. I join my prayer to that of millions of others when I turn in penitence and hope to not only wish for, but to work for, the healing of our damaged world and the deep desire that our children and grandchildren may live to see recovery and sustainability return to the beautiful world that is our home.

I would like to thank the staff of Darton, Longman and Todd for their help and support through the months of the production of this book. Their unfailing encouragement and gentle steering is, in itself, an eye-opener to an author who just writes and believes things naturally fall into place. The fact that they do relies on the hard work and good will of many people.

My wife Helen reads and suggests, and on that level alone is immensely important, but our daily walks in our Isle of Man home village and our partnership in growing fruit and vegetables and flowers in our garden, keep us ever mindful of the privilege of living on an island which is an entire UNESCO biosphere, with its sea and hills, its farmland, moorland, glens and waterfalls, its trails and pilgrim routes, and its island-dwelling people, with Celtic, Viking and British roots, now enriched by the influx of members of many nations, and of cultures all of whom contribute towards a consensus demanding a renewed effort to be catalysts for good in Nature, and to reverse the destruction of what we all hold dear.

John Mann

Principal Authors Quoted:

Pierre Teilhard de Chardin, S.J. (1881-1955): French Jesuit priest, palaeontologist, philosopher, theologian, mystic, and teacher. Probably best known for *The Phenomenon of Man*, but in the context of this book his later devotional work *Le Milieu Divin* is primarily referenced. His thoughts were drawn from his own life of prayer as well as his work and views as a scientist. He lived, worked and wrote during a critical period of the twentieth century.

Simone Weil (1909-1943): French philosopher, mystic and political activist. Her short life included significant periods of illness, and personal commitment to the reality of suffering and affliction during the inter-world war years. Her reflections on religion, spirituality and politics remain influential.

Søren Kierkegaard (1813-1855): Danish theologian, philosopher, poet, and social critic. He highlighted the importance of personal choice and commitment, and the duty to love. He valued human reality over abstract thinking.

Introduction

WHEN BROWSING THE shelves of libraries and bookshops we are all inclined to look first to the sections holding subjects that interest us, and our own bookshelves will reflect the same natural process of selection. There will be an historical aspect to this as well, amongst those whose lives can be measured by their reading at particular periods of their lives. Long has it been observed that the date of a priest's ordination could be ascertained within the space of a very few years by the authors of the theological and devotional books in his or her study. However, there is a subject today that has been growing in importance, latterly exponentially, over the past fifty and more years, that goes beyond personal preference and affects every person on this planet, every living thing, the conduct of governments, scientists, research institutions – and even theologians – from the young child starting school, learning about how and what to recycle, to the aged and fragile, whose prayers and hopes are burdened with desire that humanity may turn back from destruction and selfish gain and find the will to change its ways, and that is the health of planet Earth: our home, and that of the future of our race and the creatures, plants and the fresh water and sea life with which we share this beautiful and, as far as we know, unique planet in the universe.

The threats that exist of climate change, pollution, and environmental degradation through human activity, the uncontrolled greed for the Earth's finite resources, the extraction and burning of fossil fuels, are well known and are inexorably recorded daily. While wars rage and humans continue to inflict horrendous suffering on other humans with the immediacy of a rolling news broadcast, the long term concern of the effects of human activity is laid bare on websites, though social media, within journals, and from the well-informed comments of environmental pressure groups, by poets, artists, musicians, scientists, politicians, theologians, academics, farmers, fishers, and just about any teacher, parent and grandparent that is concerned about just what will be the condition of the Earth that this generation shall pass on to future generations. To consider this simple truth in all its aspects takes time, and for the Christian a desire to turn those considerations into prayers is a compulsion for many, and a deeply underlying concern for many more. Thus it is that the Church, in its wisdom, and its penitence for its own mistakes, has declared a period each year to do this very thing. No one is entirely untouched; no one is entirely innocent.

The Season of Creation is the newest element of the Christian Year and (to the Church of England calendar, from 2026) has been added on this Season's first Sunday, 'The Feast of God the Creator', otherwise to be known as 'The Feast of Creation in Christ'. Whilst *Festivals* of several different kinds have been added in many Christian traditions, and have varied in their importance during particular eras of the Church's history, *Seasons* have largely remained as they were formed in the early centuries. Advent and Lent are linked to the festivals of Christmas and Easter and are a format of days for their preparation, but the beginning and the end dates of the Season of Creation are linked with the concern for Creation in the Eastern and the Western traditions of Christianity, respectively. The date 1 September was proclaimed as a day of prayer for the environment by the late Ecumenical Patriarch Dimitrios I in 1989, and 4 October is the feast day of St Francis of Assisi throughout Christianity in the West. These dates span 34 days of prayer and reflection on the environment and how natural occurrences and human activity affect the world in which we live, and a festival at the Season of Creation's start to draw particular attention to its importance.

It seems appropriate to place the thoughts and prayers each year within the theme that has been chosen annually, and is generally announced by the Pope, but the process is representative of many churches and organisations passionate for the ecology and health of the planet (these organisations include Laudato Si' Movement, the World Council of Churches, the Lutheran World Federation, and the Anglican Communion). However, in this book I have chosen a broader canvas on which to suggest a period of reflection on the environment, and sought the wisdom of two French thinkers of the twentieth century to spur on the underlying feelings for the critical days in which we live. By reaching back nearly a century, I contemplate something of the scale of the issue. This is not just a contemporary matter, though as I mentioned above there are many writers engaged in illustrating the threats to life on Earth, but it is one which has affected and will continue to affect, no matter what the future holds, the attention of Christians, and those of other faiths and none, in fact the whole of God's created world. I do this also because both of these French thinkers lived and worked conscious of conflict, suffering and all the realities of human life. We are in days that witness restraint in international relations being significantly weakened, and dangerous and damaging conflicts ongoing, true dialogue dismissed or curtailed through the exercise of raw economic and military power. Informed voices from a critical period of the past speak to me, and I hope will speak to you too, as we consider their words, and dwell upon the earth, its beauty and resources, and the biblical reflections shaped by God's presence within and apart from the world in which the incarnate Christ entered at a particular moment in history, and restored humanity through the miracle of his own death and resurrection. Such is the profound and eternal truth that deepens our awareness and confirms our faith.

For each day of the 34 days of the Creation Season this book provides a biblical reference, and (with one exception, when I refer to the words of the Danish philosopher Søren Kierkegaard) a reflection from either the Jesuit priest, theologian and palaeontologist Teilhard de Chardin (1881-1955) or the extraordinarily inspirational philosopher and teacher Simone Weil (1909-1943), and often a reference to some aspect of nature that is familiar in the British and Irish countryside. By constructing each day in this way, both practical observation and theological reflection can inform each other, and the daily life of the natural environment in these islands be the gauge for a broader contemplation of the wonder of God's creation across the globe.

DAY 1 (1st September)

The Beginning

Genesis 1:1, 2

> *In the beginning God created the heaven and the earth. And the earth was without form, and void; and darkness was upon the face of the deep. And the Spirit of God moved upon the face of the waters.*

IT IS IMPOSSIBLE to think of starting a series of reflections on Creation without choosing this text, the very first two verses of the Book of Genesis, and hence also the first two verses of the whole Bible. The Christian is apt to place the presence of Christ within this thought of God, brooding in the Spirit upon the face of the earth, the waters covering it, and darkness hiding its formless void. When reading these verses in church we move swiftly to the first day of Creation and all the action which rapidly sees the sense of nothingness become a living entity. The world is created, the 'without form' becomes a distinct form, and the void a place of life.

Teilhard de Chardin from his scientific studies and anthropological understanding was writing from the backdrop of the First World War in an essay entitled, 'In the Form of Christ'.

In it he is critical of his generation of Christians whom he sees as possessing 'too extrinsic and too individualistic' an understanding of the faith they profess.[1] A century later and in the mid-2020s, in a world that is conscious of the sacrifices necessary to maintain peace and security, but also acutely aware that the environmental impact of the global industrial development is destroying the very planet that is the home of humanity, and drawn from the void by a loving God, Christians are at less risk of seeking individual escape from the dangers of world catastrophe, but also of being sufficiently coordinated in corporate action to transform a darkening and threatening world.

Teilhard wrote that,

> *In Scripture Christ is essentially revealed as invested with the power of giving the world, in his own person, its definitive form. He is consecrated for a cosmic function.*[2]

In both creation and redemption Christ's essential message through his action, as much and perhaps even more than his words, leaves humanity in general, and the Christian Church in particular, with the contemplation of a wide vision that encompasses the 'in earth' of the old form of the Lord's Prayer, much as the weaker, 'on earth' has supplanted it in modern forms. Christ's consecrated calling, so often seen as a sacrifice for the individual sinner, finds this perhaps more nebulous, but nonetheless supremely glorious,

[1]   Teilhard de Chardin, *The Hymn of the Universe*, p. 17.
[2]   Teilhard de Chardin, *The Hymn of the Universe*, p. 19.

understanding of our Lord as inspirer of the whole, the cosmic function that is his and his alone.

In taking a microscope slide and placing a drop of pond water under strong magnification, the amazing world of the microscopic organism is shown in its wonder and delicate structure. Whilst the Book of Genesis brings the cosmic scene in its magnificent sweep of all that lives and breathes and has its being, the microscopic is where the measure of the miracle of Creation is most gripping and wonderful. What no eye can see of its own strength and yet has such perfection in form and function, there is plenty to consider in de Chardin's view that Christ, through the divine power invested in him, has given the world its definitive form.

The basis of this study of the environment during thirty-four days of late summer, early autumn, is essentially a study of Christ and his impact, whilst humanity has lived not in harmony with him and each other, but at odds, trying to create a better world, in our better moments, and succeeding, often unconsciously, but sometimes deliberately and greedily, to steal for short-term gain from the bountiful resources that Christians see as both created and restored by a loving God. We begin the Creation Season with the thought and prayer that to realign human endeavour with Christ's person, investment in the created world will, in itself, bring the focus of our attention to where it should lie, in the love of God who drew life from the void.

PRAYER

Father and Lord of all Creation,
on this first day of this special Season,
we give you thanks and praise
for the beauty of the earth,
and the wonder of life in all its fullness.
Bring us through these days,
humbly and penitentially, to know our
    weakness
and to acknowledge our sinfulness,
that we may be led to a deeper sense
of Christ's abiding presence in and through
the world in which we live,
and in whose redemption of this life
we pray, in unity and love.
Amen.

DAY 2 (2nd September)

Dominion

Genesis 1:26

> *So God created man in his own image, in the image of God created he him; male and female created he them. And God blessed them, and God said unto them, Be fruitful, and multiply, and replenish the earth, and subdue it: and have dominion over the fish of the sea, and over the fowl of the air, and over every living thing that moveth upon the earth.*

THE WORD 'DOMINION' in this text is apt to make environmentalists shiver with a mixture of rage and sadness. If it is true that humanity has this level of authority over the rest of Creation, then the dire state of the planet screams out the evidence of failure. The protests against the twin evils of squandering and ill-using finite resources, and polluting pristine and delicate ecosystems, cannot be silenced, but because their effects are disproportionately affecting the poorest people on Earth, the wealthy have assumed a mask of complacency that is a barrier to action. There is nothing new in this, from

Silent Spring[3] and for some decades before, the world's ecosystem has been abused in a way that has been careless and irresponsible, but is now deliberate and arrogant. The issues have been clear for half a century, and still from a Judaeo-Christian perspective, humanity's dominion is either a misinterpretation of God's intention and gift, and these verses from Genesis chapter 1 are misunderstood, or it is a failure to acknowledge them of truly colossal proportions. One or other it must be.

Within the twenty-first century there has been a greater recognition of the place of *Homo sapiens* as an advanced animal species amongst other animal species, rather than being in a class of its own. Teilhard de Chardin as an anthropologist and archaeologist, but also as Christian and priest, formulates his theory of humanity in a special category, not so much biologically as spiritually, but within the understanding that not only is the human individual not as independent from others as humans often desire to act, but humanity is also interdependent with the whole of Creation and cannot be separated from it. This immediately locates us in a contemporary orbit, whilst maintaining the unique inner relationship with Christ that we are ever drawn towards.

'Without hesitation, as a matter of duty in a religious spirit, the soul, in the first stage of its evolution in Christ, plunges into created things.'[4]

---

[3]   Rachel Carson's classic work, published in 1962, which marked an awakening of humanity to the wholesale destruction of insect, bird and animal life through the indiscriminate and widespread use of damaging chemicals, specifically DDT, in agriculture and pest control.
[4]   Teilhard de Chardin, *The Hymn of the Universe*, p. 28.

This sentence reveals Teilhard de Chardin's belief that the place of humanity in God's plan is an entwined vision of evolving with Christ as part of the created world, not apart from it. He goes on to speak of the human soul moving to the stage of detachment from the world, but let us concentrate immediately on our duty of involvement in the created order, for this is also connected with the relationship between the active and the passive in human existence.

Taking a step or two back, as enlightenment through revelation leads us into an understanding of the world that we hadn't had before, we can see de Chardin's view that, 'Revelation CREATES spirits to the degree it enlightens them'.[5] So what of human 'dominion over the fish of the sea, and over the fowl of the air, and over every living thing that moveth upon the earth'? Surely, as enlightenment comes, the human spirit in some sense, which I can't quite define yet, is enriched, is re-created, causing the physical relationship between human and other animal to be widened, not perhaps sharply, but materially, just the same. So, the place of faith is important, but equally, the effect of intention changing makes a significant difference. But, lest we lead on from this to imagine that a human being, and humanity in general, can somehow glide over the face of the rest of Creation from this point of elected dominion, Teilhard de Chardin states, quite clearly:

We must never forget that because a man turns to God it does not mean that he no longer needs to

---

[5] Teilhard de Chardin, *The Hymn of the Universe*, p. 23.

breathe, to take nourishment – to grow in stature in every way before his fellow men.[6]

The inner change lifts the human soul, in essence by a process of growth, not only within the created order but within the fellowship of human life as well:

Thus, through the combined power of faith and intention, a new world is formed for the Christian within things, without in any way changing the features of the old.[7]

If we struggle with holding the word 'dominion', for the description of humanity's role in Creation, we may find in the concept of a human soul evolving its relationship to Creation, as it evolves its relationship with Christ, a more meaningful expression of a process of renewal and activity that is, at the same time, binding to the old physical, biological relationship, yet encountering an inner, spiritual and, to some extent, redefining state, that, as linked to the person of Jesus Christ is both *in* the world and not *of* the world in a way that needs to be teased out much further.

In one sense we can understand this in a non-hierarchical way by seeing ourselves as in some respect camouflaged within Creation, as a grayling butterfly, at rest, is hidden against heathland undergrowth, or a yellow underwing moth in an urban garden, so when they take flight the flash of colour surprises us as it lights up the insect for a few seconds before the creature comes

[6] Teilhard de Chardin, *The Hymn of the Universe*, p. 27.
[7] Teilhard de Chardin, *The Hymn of the Universe*, p. 26.

to rest once more and disappears, embracing its symbiotic relationship with the surroundings.

PRAYER

Heavenly Father,
guide our thoughts on human responsibility,
where we are failing, bring penitence;
where we act, grant wisdom;
when we plan, show us the way;
may we know when to be patient,
and when to be impatient;
above all, may your Holy Spirit determine
how we hear the voice,
and see the true beauty,
of the wonderful world in which you have
    placed us,
in Jesus Christ our Lord.
Amen.

DAY 3 (3rd September)

Offering

Genesis 4:1-5

And Adam knew Eve his wife; and she conceived, and bare Cain, and said, I have gotten a man from the Lord. And she again bare his brother Abel. And Abel was a keeper of sheep, but Cain was a tiller of the ground. And in process of time it came to pass, that Cain brought of the fruit of the ground an offering unto the Lord. And Abel, he also brought of the firstlings of his flock and of the fat thereof. And the Lord had respect unto Abel and to his offering: But unto Cain and to his offering he had not respect. And Cain was very wroth, and his countenance fell.

THE OFFERING OF part of the bounty from the earth we receive in this life, seen as a necessity for Christians, is widely recognised, whether actually at the level of a tithe, reckoned as ten per cent from the Levitical demand[8] or a self-determined amount, but a range of attitudes towards whether

---

[8] Leviticus 27:30: 'A tenth of the produce of the land, whether grain or fruit, is the Lord's, and is holy.' In Proverbs 3:9: 'Honour the Lord with your wealth, with the first fruits of all your crops.'

this in the nature of a gift, or handing over the proportion of our income which is not ours to keep, is an interesting thought, and one likely to produce a lively debate. What lies beneath this, and brings us to the Cain and Abel scenario is the place of motive. Was God's acceptance or non-acceptance of their gifts dependent on the mindset of the giver? It is most probable that this indicates the correct understanding of this text. We enter murky waters when we examine why nations, organisations and individuals give gifts to others. Without love, what is a gift worth? If a donor wishes to gain from the gift, to what extent does it devalue it? It does the same thing, and is worth no less, if given with hope of some reward. Or does it?

There is much talk today of 'soft power' whereby influence is bought for aid. It is not exactly tangible, but neither is it entirely ephemeral. It sits like an unspoken promise, or a faintly scented atmosphere waiting for someone to claim something, or for an incident to reveal an underlying truth. Cain in some way did not measure up to what God expected, whilst Abel's gift was seen as given with an open hand. Then there is the matter of the quality of what is offered. In money terms a pound is a pound, but in crops and cattle, there are better and poorer offerings that may be given.

Translating this into environmental matters for this Creation Season is complex. The interconnectedness of all things means that, all of the time, humanity must balance its impact by looking to the greater good. How impossible this is, at least to get it right at every turn. We may be able to see both the benefits and disadvantages of, for example, re-wilding beavers in some waterways in Britain and Ireland, or weighing the risks verses benefits of building nuclear power stations, but as individuals, how do we assess our influence for good or ill by living the way we do? Some issues are straightforward, many are not.

Teilhard de Chardin in considering the human relationship with the created world looks, in due course, at the soul that has plunged into interaction with the world, but has then sought detachment, 'or emergence from the world', describing this as the 'second stage of the soul's formation'.[9] He indicates that there is a phased movement, but that it can be cyclical:

> *It is not uncommon to find in the history of individual developments a distinct phase of growth … which is followed by a period of suffering and detachment … This reciprocating movement may recur several times in the course of one man's life, with a tendency always to become stabilised at a higher level, in a lesser degree of egocentrism.*[10]

The prayer for wisdom may be answered in more than one way, but clarity over motive, and the passion to do what is right in an analytical, and in as-near-as-possible objective way, makes the tragedy of Cain and Abel, which admittedly is an extreme example, an unlikely scenario. It is, however, a sobering thought that wrong motives taken to their extreme may cause great harm and leave individuals sour and even cynical.

[9] Teilhard de Chardin, *The Hymn of the Universe*, p. 29.
[10] Teilhard de Chardin, *The Hymn of the Universe*, p. 30.

PRAYER

Examine me, O Lord, in your mercy.
Reprieve the offering of myself from taint
    of pride,
bring zeal to my actions and truth to my lips
lest I fail today as I have done in the past.
Grant me your forgiveness, I pray,
and a peaceful heart and mind,
in your Son, Jesus Christ.
Amen.

DAY 4 (4th September)

Need

Genesis 41:4b-7

Pharaoh awoke.

And he slept and dreamed the second time: and, behold, seven ears of corn came up upon one stalk, rank and good. And, behold, seven thin ears and blasted with the east wind sprung up after them.

And the seven thin ears devoured the seven rank and full ears.

And Pharaoh awoke, and, behold, it was a dream.

THE PREDICTION OF seven good years of bumper harvests followed by seven years of famine, made by Joseph interpreting Pharaoh's dreams, was what extracted him from prison and gave him high standing in the country. It led to his reconciliation with his family and the establishment of their domicile in Egypt, where they were to remain until the time of Moses. The drama of these times is familiar to new generations through the musical 'Joseph and the Amazing Technicolor Dreamcoat'. The reality of wildly changeable weather patterns is now accepted as part of what the industrial world, through its massive consumption and release of carbon dioxide from long buried fossil fuels being extracted and burnt, has brought upon all peoples and all lands. To some the dangers and subsequent suffering has been far greater than to others; disproportionately this has fallen on some of the poorer nations, less able to cope and far more vulnerable to the effects.

Seven years of famine, without the Egyptian storehouses full from the wise counsel of Joseph over the previous seven years, would have meant severe problems, but the dream and the interpretation were acted upon and more than just Egypt was saved. Genesis does not go into details as to how the grain stores were filled, but one may assume that an all-powerful Pharaoh was quite capable of demanding a proportion from every producer.

Food security is high on the agenda in our own day. It is not only the threat of the climate emergency, but most countries in a position to protect themselves are harnessing their economies to a likely war situation, whence the free flow of food and raw materials is disrupted. Areas, such as north-east Africa, already vulnerable to fluctuating rainfall and high temperatures, have the added burden of years of civil war, as scarce resources are claimed by the strongest, and the weak are driven to desperate journeys from their homes to seek help elsewhere, which is not always available, as aid is nothing like as well-resourced as in previous times, and distribution ever a problem.

So Pharaoh's vision of thin grains blasted with an east wind is a timely picture of what food security looks like to those who lack it. But the big question that all of this begs is, 'How does the individual, and specifically the individual Christian, view and respond to within, spiritually, the anxieties and vulnerabilities of this world, with all the threats and fears that makes the cornered animal rear up and protect itself and its weaker members?'

Teilhard de Chardin wrote:

> *If … we step down into ourselves, we shall be horrified to find, there, beneath the man of surface relationships and reflection, an unknown – a man as yet hardly emerged from unconsciousness, still, for lack of the appropriate stimulus, no more than half-awake: one whose features, seen in the half-shadow seem to be merging into the countenance of the world.*[11]

The recognition that we are not all we would wish to be was noted by St Paul, referencing his own attempts to be what he would like himself to be in God's sight: 'For the good that I would I do not: but the evil which I would not, that I do'[12]. What Teilhard de Chardin is identifying is a deep spiritual malaise, not simply a moral or behavioural one, or in relationship terms, a sociological weakness, much as it may reveal itself as such. His description of being 'no more than half awake' is particularly telling. Little wonder that nations sleepwalk through deteriorating diplomatic relations and mutual distrust and the trading of insults, disbelief and threats to finite resources into outright war.

In nature, the survival of the fittest was seen by the early evolutionary scientists from

[11] Teilhard de Chardin, *The Hymn of the Universe*, p. 55.
[12] Romans 7:19.

Darwin onwards, to bring about the refining of a species to better survive its living conditions, be it through improved camouflage, for example, or better adapted features, such as a long proboscis for reaching deeper into a flower for the nectar, or the strength of scent to attract a mate over miles of countryside. It is just this power to dominate by being stronger or better adapted than others that has led, historically to the great empires of the world, and a trend which Jesus opposed with the law of love, as its source of operation and outlook. Joseph, it could be said, was lifted from prison and set in authority in Egypt to promote this very cause of domination, much as the story is painted in terms of salvation.

The question is, are we horrified to find, beneath the surface of our relationships, the 'half shadow' of the features of the world and its values?

PRAYER

Lord Jesus Christ,
you came among us as one to save the lost
and raise the fallen.
Teach us to see ourselves as you see us.
Awaken our senses and enlighten our eyes,
and show us what it means to truly love,
with your aching heart for justice
and compassion and mercy.
In your name we pray.
Amen.

DAY 5 (5th September)
Equality for One's Neighbour
Exodus 2:1-8

And there went a man of the house of Levi, and took to wife a daughter of Levi.

And the woman conceived, and bare a son: and when she saw him that he was a goodly child, she hid him three months.

And when she could not longer hide him, she took for him an ark of bulrushes, and daubed it with slime and with pitch, and put the child therein; and she laid it in the flags by the river's brink.

And his sister stood afar off, to wit what would be done to him.

And the daughter of Pharaoh came down to wash herself at the river; and her maidens walked along by the river's side; and when she saw the ark among the flags, she sent her maid to fetch it.

And when she had opened it, she saw the child: and, behold, the babe wept. And she had compassion on him, and said, This is one of the Hebrews' children.

Then said his sister to Pharaoh's daughter, Shall I go and call to thee a nurse of the Hebrew women, that she may nurse the child for thee?

And Pharaoh's daughter said to her, Go. And the maid went and called the child's mother.

THIS IS A story that opens issues that we may not wish to open and stirs thoughts that we would rather let lie. The Hebrew people have become strong and numerous and the Egyptians want them to be suppressed and yet useful to them. They have become enslaved and are to be kept in check. The weaker the people, the less likely to rebel, so their strength was sapped by imposing heavy labour and their capacity for improving their lot hugely reduced by removing all the male children. Inadvertently the birth of Moses and his safety brought about, ultimately, a cuckoo in the nest of the family of Pharaoh. Another example of an individual motive having far-reaching effects on a whole nation, such as we saw yesterday in the case of Joseph.

Teilhard de Chardin wishes us to dig deeper than this cause-and-effect cycle of the struggle between peoples and nations, of which much can be seen in our own day. Accepting that this is the way of the world in general, and always has been, Père Teilhard suggests we look at what is underlying this repetitive trend in human relations:

> *… it is not enough for man to throw off his self-love and live as a social being. He needs to live with his whole heart in union with the totality of the world that carries him along cosmically.*[13]

adding:

> *The man who finds his neighbour too heavy a burden must inevitably be weary already of bearing the burden of his own self.*[14]

[13]   Teilhard de Chardin, *The Hymn of the Universe*, p. 56.
[14]   Teilhard de Chardin, *The Hymn of the Universe*, p. 60.

It is undeniably the case that for humanity to assume a deeper level of communication between communities and peoples an encounter with the inner spiritual beliefs and desires of the nations must be effected. This places a huge burden on the religious leaders to enter such discussions with an openness of heart and mind that can create the milieu for progress. The potential fruit of such in-depth encounter is, however, considerable. If it is possible to find common ground amidst conflicting doctrinal beliefs – on the basis that all religious traditions seek the flourishing of human kind – even seeking the goal through the miracle of dialogue, will, in itself, create hearts, 'in union with the totality of the world' and lift the burden of weariness.

It is not insignificant that the story of Moses begins with his birth, and key to its place in the story of the Hebrew people is that its success is managed while he is in his infancy. Moses in the basket hidden in the bulrushes may have been manipulated by adults into attempting to force the hand of Pharaoh's daughter, and by so doing saving the life of the little child, but symbolically, the story corresponds thematically with Hannah and Samuel and supremely with the nativity of Christ. From the Christian perspective, the uniting factor for people of faith that brings us into harmony with a world that has been spoilt by corrupting influences is what we call 'grace'. Teilhard de Chardin defines 'grace' in these terms:

It is the unique sap that starts from the same trunk and rises up into the branches, it is the blood that courses through the veins under the impulse of one and the same heart, the nervous current that is transmitted through the limbs at the dictate of one and the same head, that mighty heart, that fruitful stock, must inevitably be Christ.[15]

Christians may enter the debate on the unity and equality of the whole human race from such a perspective; when they have done so, matters of justice and mutual support follow and flow with far-reaching consequences. They cannot unilaterally redefine international relations, but can establish an individual nation's attitude towards others, that may or may not be reciprocated. Regarding the natural world, an understanding of the grace of Christ that is defined by biological metaphors, such as suggested by Père Teilhard, assumes a delicacy in touching the physical environment which in itself is creative and life-giving.

There are those whose relationship with their surroundings is observant and attentive, and to emulate and encourage such mindful reflection is in itself metaphorically defined by placing one's vulnerable infant in a basket amongst the reeds of a river and taking the consequences. The risks are high indeed, and the outcome uncertain, but the hope is for the breaking down of a wall of opposition and the creation of a place of renewal.

[15] Teilhard de Chardin, *The Hymn of the Universe*, pp. 81, 82.

PRAYER

Heavenly Father,
we seek the grace
which holds compassion and mercy
with equality and justice.
Grant us this grace
and help us live out its consequences
in our daily lives,
through he who is its source,
even Christ our Lord.
Amen.

DAY 6 (6th September)

Hidden Springs

Exodus 15:22-25a

> *Then Moses ordered Israel to set out from the Red Sea, and they went into the wilderness of Shur. They went three days in the wilderness and found no water. When they came to Marah, they could not drink the water of Marah because it was bitter. That is why it was called Marah. And the people complained against Moses, saying, 'What shall we drink?' He cried out to the Lord; and the Lord showed him a piece of wood; he threw it into the water, and the water became sweet.*

HAVING BEEN SAVED from the Egyptian army at the Red Sea, the Hebrew people find themselves in the wilderness and short of water. All that is available is virtually undrinkable, tasting bitter, and the people started complaining to Moses. Temporarily, the situation was corrected as Moses was shown by God a particular tree that had healing properties, and by throwing this into the water, it sweetened it. But they needed to press on to somewhere with a more reliable water source. This they found at Elim, which, we are told held twelve springs of swater and seventy palm trees. Much better!

The thought of springs of water and trees reminds me of some striking pictures that the Danish philosopher and theologian Søren Kierkegaard uses at the beginning of his book *Works of Love* published in 1847. He speaks of the 'hidden life' of love within us as being in the 'inward depths', and still 'has an unfathomable connection with the whole of existence'. He tries to explain at length what he means by this, in these words:

> *As the quiet lake is grounded darkly in the deep spring, which no eyes see, so is human love mysteriously grounded in God's love [...]*
>
> *As the quiet lake invites you to look at it, but by its dark reflection prevents your looking down through it, so the mysterious origin of love in the love of God prevents you from seeing its source; if you think you see it, then you are deceived by a reflection, as if that which merely conceals the deeper source were the true source. As the ingenious cover, placed over a treasure for the express purpose of absolutely concealing the treasure, looks like the bottom of the receptacle, so that reflection which but conceals something even deeper, looks deceptively like the deep bottom.*
>
> *[...] so love, however quiet it is in its concealment, is ever flowing.* [16]

This picture of the still lake being fed by a hidden flowing spring beneath it, being as our love fed by that of God, is one I find to be very helpful, particularly as we see the care

[16] Søren Kierkegaard, *Works of Love* (Copenhagen, 1847; Princetown University Press, 1949), pp. 8, 9.

and compassion of those supporting others through illness revealing a depth of self-offering that is affecting us all. But Kierkegaard expands on what he means by the 'mirror of darkness' too. As we look into the still lake with a mirror-like surface, it is impossible for the on-looker to see into the depths. What we see is ourselves reflected back, and he describes this as deceiving us. In other words what Kierkegaard is saying to me is, 'Don't try and look into the heart of another to see the source of their love – you know that it is there. Look within yourself to the hidden springs that God supplies for you, and drink of it.' God has placed within us all this capacity, as he brought the Israelites to the place of twelve springs and seventy palm trees.

Kierkegaard also has wonderful thoughts about the tree and its fruits and leaves, and how we see and hear and experience love. But that is for another day …

PRAYER

Lord Jesus,
we know that there are
hidden springs of love
found within human hearts,
may mine be ever more
drawn out by you
and not obscured by the rock
of my selfishness.
Break the stone

and release the spring,
so may I live for others
and most of all,
for you.
Amen.

DAY 7 (7th September)

The Mountaintop

Exodus 19:1-6a

MOSES' ASCENT OF Mount Sinai is one of the defining moments of the history of God's people. It brought the law to people, but it in a really important sense brought perspective too. Mountain top experiences are good for getting things in scale. Whatever may loom large on the plain has a way of diminishing in importance when viewed from above, especially high above. The contrary is also true, that things seen close-up that do not appear to be particularly important, when seen in their thousands from afar may seem far more threatening and more of a long-term problem.

One of the historical quotations that I remember from school days was that by Winston Churchill describing T. E. Lawrence: 'He was indeed a dweller upon the mountain tops where the air is cold, crisp and rarefied, and where the view on clear days commands all the Kingdoms of the world and the glory of them.' I recall this description inspiring me at the time with a strange sense of admiration mixed with energising a wish to experience this sensation too. Physically the climb and gaining height and view are one thing, but detachment and vision are equally potent.

On the sixth day of the Creation Season, this is providing a moment to pause and take stock; the thought of Moses ascending the mountain and returning to find the people already losing their way, causing him incandescent anger, and its parallel of visionary thoughts as to how to save the planet meeting inertia when those life-saving plans hit the fan of short-term economic targets and the greed of wealthy nations, is not an unreal one. Nevertheless, catching and holding a vision, and putting a marker down that keeps one conscious of it, such as Moses carried on two tablets of stone, is a vital ingredient in a new endeavour, and, strangely too, a closeted safeguard against losing heart. In Teilhard de Chardin's essay on the interior life, left in the English translation with the title *Le Milieu Divin,* he has a short section titled, 'Detachment through Action'. In it he writes:

> *The more nobly a man wills and acts the more avid he becomes for great and sublime aims to pursue. He will no longer be content with family, country and the remunerative aspect of his work. He will want wider organisation to create, new paths to blaze, causes to uphold, truths to discover, an ideal to cherish and defend.*[17]

In Britain and Ireland, and elsewhere as well, of course, some of our most mysterious and awe-inspiring creatures and plants are to be found in high mountainous areas. Soaring eagles, tiny alpine flowers, insects adapted to extreme conditions, thrive in the 'cold, crisp and rarefied' atmosphere of places that would leave other living things desiccated, torn from their roots, unable to move, feed or make their home. The wild can find us at our best, but meeting its threats are part of the adventure, and whether or not we feel closer to God when physically there is a question that any of us may ask, and answer subjectively, but metaphorically at least to dwell on the mountain top is to be inspired, energised, and to come close to the ground of our being and be conscious of all the needs and desires of our lives. As we consider the world in its beauty and wonder, but under threat and damaged, let us rest today with the vision from the high ground before us.

[17]   Teilhard de Chardin, *Le Milieu Divin*, p. 72.

PRAYER

Heavenly Father,
on this day we come in slow steps
upon the mountainside, reaching ever
    upwards.
As we gain height, lift our eyes from our
unsteady feet to the peak.
Renew our vision and inspire our efforts,
not to gain glory for ourselves,
but to acknowledge the glory that is yours,
and reflected in the world around us.
May our contemplation be through
your Son Jesus Christ in whom we pray.
Amen.

DAY 8 (8th September)
Darkness and Light
Joshua 2:5

> *And when it was time to close the gate at dark, the men went out. Where the men went I do not know. Pursue them quickly, for you can overtake them.*

AT TIMES EVEN in Britain and Ireland we have needed rain, and needed it badly. Not on the scale of places on Earth where it hardly ever rains, but, on the other hand, our countryside is used to having a heavy dose of precipitation most months of the year, and when we don't get it the extent of the parched ground has become obvious, with the grass turning brown and cracks opening ever wider in paths throughout the countryside. It is hard to imagine that there were places impassable because of mud at other times, such is the contrast. An equally telling contrast is that between light and darkness, and that too can be experienced in the very depths of the natural world.

The writer Tim Robinson, who died of COVID-19 on 3 April 2020, just two weeks after his wife Máiréad had also died, moved from Hampstead to the far west of Ireland in 1972, and would have soon learnt all about rain, the vagaries of the Atlantic Ocean that pounds that side of Ireland, and life on an off-shore island. He and Máiréad lived on the largest of the Aran islands; an incredibly different lifestyle to that they had left in London (though they did retain a flat there). Nicholas Allen, writing Tim's obituary, which appeared in the *Guardian* at the time, sets the scene of life at their house on the Aran islands:

> '*No matter what the talk, this was a hard place to keep the mind still, the clouds scudding across the far mountains, squalls racing the water. At the back was a cluttered hall and a bedroom whose doors opened to a garden hedged against the salt winds of the Atlantic. On spring days Tim and Máiréad lay in bed and waited for the robin to feed from the dish of crumbs they kept beside the bed.*'

They eventually left Aran, and went to live on the mainland of Connemara, and Tim became increasingly well-known as one of the finest Irish writers of his generation, recording many historical and cultural features of the area that they had made their home. Five years prior to their deaths, due to health reasons they returned to their flat in Hampstead and lived there until dying, as I say, just days apart.

I have been dipping into one of Tim's books. It has a pool with waterlily leaves on the front cover, reminding me of the vital need of water for life, and why Ireland is so green, for it only very rarely has a year when it is baked brown like the south of England, and even then not as universally – there always seems to be a lake around the next corner. The book is called, *The Last Pool of Darkness*, but, in fact, refers not to water, but to light. The title is a quotation from the philosopher Ludwig

Wittgenstein, who in 1948 left the University City of Cambridge to spend time at a friend's holiday cottage in the hamlet of Rosroe, in the area of Ireland's western seaboard that Tim and Máiréad were to make their home more than twenty years later. Wittgenstein remarked thus, *I can only think clearly in the dark, and in Connemara I have found one of the last pools of darkness in Europe.*

Darkness and light appear in the verse from the second chapter of Joshua taken as today's text. The Hebrew spies in Jericho are escaping with Rahab's help under the cover of darkness. Without it she could not have managed to slip them past the guards and into safety.

The deep darkness which Wittgenstein sought at the end of Europe – at the end of an Irish peninsula sticking out into the Atlantic Ocean – is an unfound, lonely darkness that speaks of undisturbed opportunity for thought, but normally we would consider somewhere *light* as revealing what we want to see and understand. But for the philosopher this was not a *state* of darkness, it was a *'pool of darkness'*, in other words a place of still contemplation, unaffected by human presence.

Tim Robinson's thought of using not only Wittgenstein's words as a title for his book, but with a picture of serenity to accompany them, suggests to me how the 'pool of darkness' reveals things by making the tiniest glimpses, of the faintest of light, like the most insignificant ripple on the face of an otherwise still lake. Wittgenstein looked into what cannot reveal, to make more obvious the things hardest to see.

There are moments in the spiritual life when it is worth remembering this thought, without needing to go to the ends of the world to find it.

We may experience goodness, even as we stare into evil, and strengthen hope, even as we look at what is darkest and most forbidding; for as a situation in life that metaphorically switches off its safety-lit exit signs, with their little green running person, what remains is what aids us to survive: the voice of a friend whom the gloom has prevented us from seeing, the helping hand of a stranger who holds us tight and dispels the pool of darkness, the realisation that Christ is closer to us than we recognised before. The minutest shafts of light are seen when we least expect them, when our eyes are focused and our minds alert. Through this and every crisis may our eyes be clear to see; as we most dearly need them to be.

PRAYER

Holy Spirit,
truth divine,
cast light,
we pray,
where darkness
engulfs us,
and refresh,
what is barren
and dry,
with living water,
as given,
by Christ alone.
Amen.

DAY 9 (9th September)

When Will We Learn?

Job 8:11-14

> *'Can papyrus grow where there is no marsh? Can reeds flourish where there is no water? While yet in flower and not cut down, they wither before any other plant. Such are the paths of all who forget God; and the hope of the godless shall perish. Their confidence is gossamer, a spider's house their trust.'*

THESE WORDS ARE spoken by Bildad the Shuhite to Job, bidding him to repent; seeking where he or his children have been at fault. Such is a comforter for Job. It was within the culture of the times that if there was ill health or some disaster befell an individual, the cause was lain at the door of the sin of that individual, or that of a close connection, probably, as in this case, the children. The picture that Bildad uses here of a dried-up marsh is one so startlingly contemporary it is hard to imagine just how long ago these words were written. Today we would not link a random personal failing with a corresponding random disaster; that direct correlation has long since been disconnected. However, the reason for floods in one place and drought in another is more widely as a result of human activity causing climate change. The patterns of climate change have been unpredictable, but whatever computer models of possible changes in future weather patterns are used, none suggest good news or are encouraging us to think that Nature will simply absorb the abuse to its systems and return to pre-industrial levels of air and sea temperatures. We have known this for a long time, and not learnt the lesson.

I have a document called an 'Ecological Audit for Local Churches'. It gives advice on how one should assess the Church facilities, looking at our use of paper, possibilities for conserving energy, directions to environment-friendly cleaning products and advice on the use of glass and china for food and drink rather than disposable items – making the point that, 'Breaking the habits of a "disposable culture" is a vital step in creating a sustainable society'. It goes on to talk of community projects that the Church should involve itself in, and that we should pursue a detailed Church and Community audit. It speaks too of the need for regular preaching and teaching on environmental issues. It asks questions about how much we recycle and whether or not we are embracing car-sharing amongst those going to church.

Then it starts to examine how we are lobbying politicians, opening our eyes to the natural world, encouraging us to plant trees and leave part of the church grounds for wildlife, and supporting campaigns that apply pressure on governments to embrace green projects. It asks questions about the Church's ethical investments, and presses us to consider the debt that poor countries owe the rich, as well as pouring scorn on the greed of Western consumers which is destroying the environment of the poor. It concludes with considering the theological implications of how we live and urges us to read the signs of the times in terms of the ecological change that is affecting the planet. All we may say is the message that is coming to us in these days of climate change and the seeking of a carbon neutral economy.

And the date on the 'Ecological Audit for Local Churches' is June 1990. Thirty-six years ago. I found it at the bottom of a box of old Church papers and booklets.

The River Jordan that runs from its various sources high in the mountains around Mount Hermon and flows into and out of the Sea of Galilee and south to the Dead Sea is an example itself of a watercourse in crisis, as extraction of fresh water has slowed its flow and lowered the levels of both the Sea of Galilee and the Dead Sea. It was in this river, in another age, that Jesus was himself baptised. Baptism was taking place amongst the reeds and the flowering water plants at the river's edge, waving in the breeze and shading the water and its creatures, such as in the days of the infant Moses in the Nile, but drying marshes spell death, and flooded crops in other areas are equally lost. Yet, as Teilhard de Chardin puts it:

> *Who can fail to perceive the great symbolic gesture of baptism in [the] general history of matter? Christ immerses himself in the waters of Jordan, symbol of the forces of the earth. These he sanctifies. And as*

he emerges, in the words of Gregory of Nyssa, with the water which runs off his body he elevates the whole world.[18]

PRAYER

Heavenly Father,
may we share the gift of water
as we share the gift of life,
in Christ your Son,
who has saved us,
and through his Spirit
sanctified us for his service
and for life itself.
Amen.

---

[18] Teilhard de Chardin, *Le Milieu Divin*, p. 110.

DAY 10 (10th September)

Ask the Animals

Job 12:7-10

But ask the animals, and they will teach you; the birds of the air, and they will tell you; ask the plants of the earth, and they will teach you; and the fish of the sea will declare to you. Who among all these does not know that the hand of the Lord has done this? In his hand is the life of every living thing and the breath of every human being.

THE TWELFTH CHAPTER of the Book of Job declares the thought that it is only when humanity is in trouble that men and women cast around for where the problems lie, and recognises that sobering and irritating fact that the wicked often prosper. There is an exasperation in reaching this conclusion, but history is inclined to support it, as tyrants and dictators, and any who misuse power granted to them democratically for their own ends and to bolster their egos, often forge ahead at the expense of those who can do nothing about it. They crush opposition and write their own story. In our own day, the use of social media as well as the more traditional forms of propaganda feed the growth of the problem. What Job then struggles with is the unexpectedness of God's action in the midst of all that is happening, in fact he cannot explain what are the principles upon which God works.

In verses 7 to 10 the witness of created things is brought to bear. Ask the animals and the birds, ask the plants and the fish – they will all declare the same thing, this is how God has created things and has put life into every living creature, for the strong to overpower and dominate the weak. Nature is indeed red in tooth and claw.[19] As Job struggles to understand these things and interpret what is happening to himself, we might like to dwell also on why we find this so difficult to comprehend. Are we as the animals and the birds, the plants and the fish? Do we act towards each other and the rest of Creation as the tyrant and dictator, or as the elected one who cannot handle the power granted to us? What is the reality? This is as much a philosophical question as a theological one, and I turn to Simone Weil for her wisdom:

We live in a world of unreality and dreams. To give up our imaginary position at the centre, to renounce

---

[19]   The words 'red in tooth and claw' come from Alfred Lord Tennyson's poem 'In Memoriam A. H. H.', 1850. The quotation comes in Canto 56 and refers to someone:

> *'Who trusted God was love indeed*
> *And love Creation's final law –*
> *Tho' Nature, red in tooth and claw*
> *With ravine, shriek'd against his creed –'*

'Tooth and claw' was already in use as a phrase denoting wild nature by Tennyson's day.

it, not only intellectually but in the imaginative part of our soul, that means to awaken to what is real and eternal, to see the true light and hear the true silence. A transformation then takes place at the very roots of our sensibility in our immediate reception of sense impressions and psychological impressions. It is a transformation analogous to that which takes place in the dusk of evening on a road, where suddenly we discern as a tree what we had at first seen as a stooping man; or where we suddenly recognise as a rustling of leaves what we thought at first was whispering voices. We see the same colours, we hear the same sounds but not in the same way.[20]

Both Teilhard de Chardin and Simone Weil were acutely analytical, reflective and fearless. Neither would shun a difficult conclusion to an intellectual quandary. Job appears to join them in the text for today in drawing himself from the centre to a place of unity with the whole created order, working on the same principles and the same outcomes. We may find comfort in this outlook, or may feel distinctly uncomfortable and out of control. Herein lies a point of contention in contemporary views on the environment. It touches also the policies and protocols that are put in place to define the way biospheres are established, and, for example, how rewilding and other projects are set up. To protect one species almost inevitably means potentially suppressing

[20]   Simone Weil, *Waiting on God*, pp. 98, 99. The quotation is from a section titled 'Love of the Order of the World', under the chapter heading, 'Forms of the Implicit Love of God'.

another, though the real gem of a project is when a restored ecosystem encourages more than one organism and creates something rare out of something which is common, and possibly also degraded.

Dwelling on Simone Weil's particular understanding of moving from a central and controlling role (from having 'dominion', as expressed in Genesis chapter 1 and in Psalm 8), there is something very attractive in the thought that it allows us to see things as they are, rather than what we think we see. I find this very helpful in holding together what appears as a directive of responsibility for the life of the whole planet, if not a God-given control, which one might well claim from a biblical perspective, because a voluntary diminishing of our feel for control, or in Simone Weil's language, to 'give up our imaginary position at the centre, to renounce it, not only intellectually but in the imaginative part of our soul', is actually a great gain. This *feels* right, it *feels* Christian, shedding something, refining life, for a better sight of ourselves and what we are doing, and not doing.

PRAYER

Creator God, consciously, and
in love, we see what is around us.
In both what is ugly and what is beautiful,
help us to see things as they are
and not as we imagine them to be.
Keep our eyes clear and true

and our hearts and minds tuned
to the earth and its creatures,
one with us in all that you have made
in and through Jesus Christ our Lord.
Amen.

DAY 11 (11th September)

Humanity's Adoration

Psalm 19

> *The heavens are telling the glory of God*
> *and the firmament proclaims his handiwork.*
> *One day pours out its song to another*
> *and one night unfolds knowledge to another.*
> *They have neither speech nor language*
> *and their voices are not heard,*
> *Yet their sound has gone out into all lands*
> *and their words to the ends of the world.*

THE SOUND OF birdsong is said to have been louder during the lockdown period of the pandemic in 2020. Was it louder, or were we more attuned to it, in the relative quiet of those days? It was a particularly beautiful and sunny spring, and maybe that helped too, but the Psalmist of Psalm 19 is not thinking of actual noise, song or speech anyway; the author taps into that part of our understanding that realises when our mental and emotional wavelength is reached by the natural world around us. The fact that God put it there is not in doubt, the only important message of the psalm is that this accepted truth should be a cause for human adoration.

Just after Easter in 2020 when we were able to walk a certain distance from our homes, my wife and I were rambling from our home in Swanage along part of the Dorset coastal path. I wrote a blog the following day which ran:

Walking yesterday afternoon, a woman who waited for us in a gap on the path, expressed the view, often heard in these days, of what glory there is about us. There was no need to say more, as from where we stood, the cowslips and orchids at our feet, the hills around us and the blue sky above, indeed, every sight and sound declared the glory of God.

At home, the apple blossom is upon the old rectory Bramley tree, while just a few of last September's stored apples remain on the wooden shelves in the garage. They are still edible, and sweet with sitting the winter long. The tree almost certainly pre-dates the house, and in its shade many a story has been told and thought pondered. It gives good value for the space it takes, and its roots spread wide in search of the water and anchorage it needs.

Such a sign of nature's permanence in a tree that outlives us, is balanced by the fragile egg in the nest or swiftly fading flower, as early spring moves to late spring and onward to summer. The daffodils and narcissi are finished, all but the late and fragrant variety called 'cheerfulness', that has managed in previous years to slip into Easter decorations when they have been needed late April, in one of those years when it seemed Easter would never come. But here we are with the festival passed, and a strange year when holidays are over but there is little outward change. It is all very odd.

The birds are still nesting though, and carrying on as if nothing were amiss. Guillemots and razorbills, shags and herring gulls, with fulmars wheeling above, are nesting all along the cliff ledges from the Tilly Whim Caves to Durlston Head; the small birds whirring busily across the sea, intent on feeding their young. Further out a dozen gannets fly in formation, no doubt also in search of food.

Lying in a woodland path a piece of shell of the egg of a song thrush presents its speckled blue reminder of new birth, and the filling of the dappled-lit undergrowth of a forest floor with the lush growth of spring; dogs mercury, wild garlic, bluebell and wood anemone. From hidden in the thickets comes the sound of birdsong, and above, the pale green of opening beech leaves contrasts so perfectly with the deep cobalt of bluebell and the cloudless sky.

In a few brief weeks it will have died back, and the mystery which we know of as spring in England will have passed for another year, but, thank God, we have it for now, its very transient beauty filling our hearts with joy; as we treasure every glimpse, and, though there is neither word nor language, we hold within receptive ears every note of song.

I am reminded of the beautiful spring and summer of 1914 before the outbreak of the First World War, and how well it is painted in Vera Brittain's *Testament of Youth*. We know too of the horrors of War and the destruction of human life and everything that sustains it, but sounds of the natural world go out to all, without voice or words, but reverberating through all life to the glory of God, and continue to cast a judgement on human greed and wickedness.

PRAYER

Merciful God,
in faith we look for you
in the world around us.
You grant us a sight that lifts our souls to you,
which, even in the passing days of the seasons,
new life, its flowering, fruition and fading,
therein lies the glory of eternity,
spelt out in the transitory stages of this life.
Keep us ever alive to its reality
and grateful in its acceptance,
through Jesus Christ our Lord.
Amen.

DAY 12 (12th September)

Be Present

Psalm 24

The earth is the Lord's and all that fills it,
the compass of the world and all who dwell
therein.
For he has founded it upon the seas
and set it firm upon the rivers of the deep.
'Who shall ascend the hill of the Lord,
or who can rise up in his holy place?'
'Those who have clean hands and a pure heart,
who have not lifted up their soul to an idol,
nor sworn an oath to a lie;
'They shall receive a blessing from the Lord,
a just reward from the God of their salvation.'
Such is the company of those who seek him,
of those who seek your face, O God of Jacob.
Lift up your heads, O gates;
be lifted up, you everlasting doors;
and the King of glory shall come in.
'Who is the King of glory?'
'The Lord, strong and mighty,
the Lord who is mighty in battle.'
Lift up your heads, O gates;
be lifted up, you everlasting doors;
and the King of glory shall come in.
'Who is this King of glory?'
'The Lord of hosts,
he is the King of glory.'

THIS PSALM IS one in which being *present* is all important. It is in occupying the space that is holy that the worshipper receives the reward. The Psalmist brings us to understand the nature of the place first. It is the earth in all its fullness, and the great bodies of water, from the sea to a mighty flood. The physicality of this concept of God's presence is unavoidable. Ascend the hill, stand in the holy place with clean hands and a pure heart, foreswear vanity and deceit and seek the Lord's face.

This psalm brings to our attention an aspect of human connection with God's creation that is not much observed today: attentiveness that is in some degree sacramental. The clean hands and pure heart chime with this thought, that within the world around us we can find the holy places and the heights, that we have mentioned already. Simone Weil speaks of something that is observed in these terms:

> *One of the principal truths of Christianity, a truth that goes almost unrecognised today, is that the looking is what saves us. The bronze serpent was lifted up so that those who lay maimed in the depths of degradation should be saved by looking upon it.*[21]

There are a number of biblical passages that involve people being invited to 'come and see'. When John the Baptist sent his disciples to Jesus to find out if he were the one who was to come or not, Jesus replied by showing them the evidence of their own eyes. A disciple asks where Jesus is

[21] Simone Weil, *Waiting on God*, p. 125.

staying and he is told to 'come and see'. Training our eyes to see properly is part of what caring for God's Creation involves. Humanity has the power to destroy itself and the planet it lives on. Observation is necessary if we are to truly respect and value it.

The smallest of things can teach us the most when handled, and presented by a priest or other spiritual leader. As Simone Weil puts it: 'At the centre of the Catholic religion a little piece of formless matter is found, a little piece of bread.'[22] Contemporary celebrations of the Eucharist emphasise that inclusion in the sacrament involves the bread and wine shared, as ever, but also partaking in the whole undertaking – fully and with attentiveness – as, generally the priest is facing the congregation across the altar/table, and every gesture is drawing the eyes and attention to what is happening upon it. Anglicans once penitentially knelt during the Book of Common Prayer Eucharistic Prayer, now they stand and observe, uplifted and one with the 'celebrant' (now declared the 'president') who is simply presiding over the ceremony of thanksgiving, remembrance and unity in which all partake.

Psalm 24 emphasises the arrival of the King. There is procession and celebration and clearing of the way. It is a psalm that has always been connected with the Festival of the Ascension of Christ, and is now generally recited or sung at Evensong on the eve of Ascension Day. The eyes are clear, the heart tuned to God, the sight is concentrated on the glory that is coming. However, the opening of the psalm places the

[22] Simone Weil, *Waiting on God*, p. 130.

Creation absolutely with God, and it has a majesty of its own, from lofty mountains to crashing seas, and who has not been inspired by the song of the skylark, ascending and descending over a summer meadow? Even those whose eyesight is not good can have an inner feel for the energy and capacity of nature to inspire and lift the heart to its Maker.

Yet as Simone Weil emphasises, it takes just a tiny morsel of matter to symbolically unite us all in the death and resurrection of Christ, through the Spirit's presence and the Father's gift of life. So, today is a day for training one's eye to see the created world as a window through which, with the inner interpretation granted by grace, to glimpse the author of our being, and hope for our life, even for eternity.

PRAYER

Christ Jesus,
Prophet, Priest and King,
Lord of all things
and our daily companion.
Have mercy on us as we approach
your kingly throne, in faith and love.
Amen.

DAY 13 (13th September)

The Voice

Psalm 29

Ascribe to the Lord, you powers of heaven,
ascribe to the Lord glory and strength.
Ascribe to the Lord the honour due to his name;
worship the Lord in the beauty of holiness.
The voice of the Lord is upon the waters;
the God of glory thunders;
the Lord is upon the mighty waters.
The voice of the Lord is mighty in operation;
the voice of the Lord is a glorious voice.
The voice of the Lord breaks the cedar trees;
the Lord breaks the cedars of Lebanon;
He makes Lebanon skip like a calf
and Sirion like a young wild ox.
The voice of the Lord splits the flash of
lightning;
the voice of the Lord shakes the wilderness;
the Lord shakes the wilderness of Kadesh.
The voice of the Lord makes the oak trees writhe
and strips the forests bare;
in his temple all cry, 'Glory!'
The Lord sits enthroned above the water flood;
the Lord sits enthroned as king for evermore.
The Lord shall give strength to his people;
the Lord shall give his people the blessing of
peace.

A LINE FROM the Ode to a Nightingale, that I learnt at school, runs:'*In some melodious plot/ Of beechen green, and shadows numberless*[23]. It describes the location of Keats' nightingale, and the place of a particular perspective on a world made glorious by sunshine through springtime leaves below a deep blue sky. *Komorebi*, I have learnt, is a Japanese word used to describe the scattered light that filters through when sunlight shines through trees, and seems to fit this experience. It is just one of the wonders of the countryside that we may experience in a single moment, in glorious weather; others, many much more dramatic, appear in the psalms. At the end of the Common Worship prayer for Psalm 29, we beseech Christ to '*open our eyes to see the vision of your [God's] glory*', as the author pours forth one picture after another of the wonder and power of the natural world. The psalm itself ascribing to nature the voice of the Lord.

Keats literally heard the sound of the nightingale; what we hear in the understanding of the psalmist, again in the words of the concluding prayer, is the music of the Lord's voice, in special moments that are just as potently glorious, but bound in the feel of the air, the scent of the wood, the sight of light and shadow, and the flickering movement of sunshine, glittering from the pale green of newly emerged leaves. All is fresh: air, light, leaf and sky. We don't need analysis, just the right angle and a mind ready to, '*Fade far away, dissolve, and*

[23] *Poems of John Keats*, Selected and with an Introduction by Claire Tomalin (Penguin Classics, 2009), p. 35, stanza 1.

quite forget/ What thou among the leaves hast never known,/ ... "[24]

What Keats found, that mid-May woodland day, was to be transported by beauty to a place where his and all the '[...] *weariness, the fever, and the fret/ Here where men sit and hear each other groan*'[25] had vanished in the bliss of the nightingale's song. The music of the Lord's voice in Psalm 29 is a proclamation not of a sound so beautiful that all is forgotten, but a voice of glorious might that gives strength and blessing, ascribing the powers of Heaven to the action and capacity of God's shaking and intent; a message conveyed from thundering seas to mighty mountains, that all this is held in the palm of God's hand.

St Patrick, whom I don't think would have sat easily with Keats' drug-like capitulation to beauty, picked up a powerful sense of God's protection and reassurance, reflected in the world around him, in his famous 'Breastplate', in which he sees himself literally as binding to himself the Trinity, and all that the Triune God is, as armour to the soul that frets and weakens in the very path of life itself. *'The Lord shall give his people the blessing of peace'*, ends the morning psalm today, and yet begins the day in the confidence that, as the new dawn appears, and the sunlight fills the sky from 93 million miles away, it is more than warm, dappled light and beauty that take possession of our souls, but the very love of the Father; the gift of his crucified and risen Son, and the power of the Spirit, promised to his Church and felt and known at Pentecost.

[24] Ibid stanza 3.
[25] Ibid.

A new day; a new binding on all that God holds out to us: creation, redemption and sanctification. We wait and watch and pray with those first disciples, and the women who were amongst Christ's most blessed and loving friends. We pray that we may know once more, today, their confidence and their hope.

PRAYER

Father,
as we listen to your voice in Creation,
we see its operation and know its power.
In awe we stand before an unknown future,
observing the changes
wrought by human activity
upon the planet that is our home.
Whilst the nightingale sings, the
vastness of the world's ecosystems
dwarfs our attention to a single bird,
symbol of what we are in danger of losing,
let us listen to your voice,
and obey your commands,
and turn and live, in Jesus Christ our Lord.
Amen.

DAY 14 (14th September)

Loneliness

Psalm 102:7, 8

SOMETIMES IT IS that the natural world resonates with our mood in a very telling way. We may not even be directly conscious of it, whilst enjoying it all the same, as we feel the sun on our faces or a breeze lifts us and we breathe deeply after hours in a stuffy room. On other occasions we can connect with some aspect of Creation deliberately and perhaps repetitively, constantly going to the same place where we know we shall feel comfortable, under trees or beside the sea, or wherever, and embracing aspects of each season as it develops through the course of the year. The sight of the first snowdrop is amongst my highlights.

It can work the other way too, as we seek to describe to someone how we feel, we may take the example of a soaring bird of prey or the delicacy of a spider's web, wet with dew, for feeling energised, on the one hand, and still with an inner sense of being drenched in peace, on the other. The psalmist who penned the words of verses 7 and 8 of Psalm 102 knew loneliness, and the words are apt and telling. If loneliness gives the overall theme of these two verses, then the specific examples from the birds mentioned illuminate issues that this author experienced. A vulture in the wilderness is a contradiction in terms, for the vulture will appear where there are pickings of food, not where there is, effectively, nothing. An owl, 'haunting ruins', may roost there, but the image of it gliding silently ghost-like across the landscape searching for prey is a more apt image. Dozens of sparrows chattering in a bush or nesting as a colony in holes and cracks in the slates of a roof, is much more the scene than a single sparrow 'upon the housetop'.

Yet loneliness is a feature of Western society in our day, and has been for some decades, with the rise of individualism and the breakdown of community life and of extended families living closely together. Local neighbourliness, with shared values of individuals and families with similar lifestyles living and working largely in harmony with one another is still experienced, but now is likely to be the subject of note and even surprise where it is found. The bright spot of committed social activity, which anecdotally may have been considered eroded, we may say has been boosted for a number of reasons, such as the Foodbank and schemes to help the homeless and refugee, but the underlying cause for this need rather underlines the premise that society has become progressively less equitable, and the isolation of poverty adds to its downward spiral of distress. Has this style of living also contributed to the environmental decay? The near ubiquitous popularity of car travel, certainly, especially when single occupancy has exacerbated the trend. We have become a fragmented people, with traditional bonds being weakened, and sometimes removed altogether. Teilhard de Chardin would have seen this trend developing even in his day, but more especially recognised its inner, spiritual malaise. The underlying similarity of people, however dispersed and divided they may become, is never lost. When we regard the nature of God himself, and in his transcendence, so far distant from us, the beauty and the comfort is that at the same time as feeling far off we are experiencing the intimacy of Christ's presence. This is more than helpful, it is crucial to a sense of oneness (that unity being in the bonds of love), however broken and crying out for healing may be the human relationships that draw our attention day by day.

> *[...] all created things, every one of them, cannot be looked at, in their nature and action, without the same reality being found in their innermost being – like sunlight in the fragments of a broken mirror – one beneath its multiplicity, unattainable beneath its proximity and spiritual beneath its materiality[...] It is precisely because he is at once so deep and yet so akin to an extension less point that God is infinitely near and dispersed everywhere.*[26]

[26] Teilhard de Chardin, *Le Milieu Divin*, p. 114.

PRAYER

Lord Jesus Christ,
the same yesterday, today and for ever,
grant us to know that,
even in our lonely times,
we are one in reaching to you in transcendence
and resting in your intimacy,
in love.
Amen.

DAY 15 (15th September)

Imagining Heaven

Psalm 104

Bless the Lord, O my soul.
O Lord my God, how excellent is your greatness!
You are clothed with majesty and honour,
wrapped in light as in a garment.
You spread out the heavens like a curtain
and lay the beams of your dwelling place in the waters above.
You make the clouds your chariot
and ride on the wings of the wind.
You make the winds your messengers
and flames of fire your servants.
You laid the foundations of the earth,
that it never should move at any time.

THIS GREAT PSALM of Creation, extolling its wonders and the majesty of God, the founder, builds its structure around that accepted understanding. The heavens, or the sky, are like a piece of fabric high above us, higher again is a heavenly sea within which are great beams which support the dwelling place of God. Clouds are chariots, the winds circulating like wings, upon which walk the heavenly spirits and from which issue flames and light. It is a powerful metaphor for the glory, that is beyond our imagination, in which God dwells. Picture it, as you like! Below this is what we know, the earth and all that dwells in it.

If one's capacity for wonder is not exhausted at this stage, then it will touch every living thing upon the face of the planet. All is related to the one who built it, and continues to work in the world. This puts an interesting perspective on the concept of humanity holding dominion or even responsibility for all living things, with the birds of the air, the fish in the sea and everything that moves upon the face of the earth. There is awe and wonder even within the primitive spatial understanding of Creation. There is not simply our need to preserve the natural environment for ourselves, we are stewards of God's beautiful and complex creation, and, whether our understanding is exacting and scientific or moral, or poetic, or emotional, we relate what we touch and see each day to the wisdom of God who, in love, made it all.

Watching our grandson with a caterpillar or worm creeping over his hand, as he turns it, keeping the creature from falling and looking at it closely, one is reminded of the wonder in a child's mind, yet as adults, though we can never quite recapture that sense of discovery, as we cannot un-know what we know, nevertheless, we can cultivate a renewed sense of awe and mystery as we look deeper into how and why what we observe is reflecting the mind of the Creator. We speak of 'creation in love' to sum up why the world came into being out of the formless void. This is thinking of the Creation on the mega level, whilst Patrick, my younger grandson, with his worm in his hand, is studying at the micro level. The wonder in each case may be of a different order, but the lesson for all who seek to find in nature a reference to God is that not only is beauty in the eye of the beholder, but to some extent, the underlying truth is too. Evidence can be presented, but in faith we are no further on, nor any way behind those who envisioned the heavens as a garment, and the angels, of such brilliance, like flames of fire.

The capacity that the physical structure of our world has to show forth the spiritual element, reflecting the love in which it was made, and continues to be made, provides a sacredness to our desire to stop the destruction of habitats and species that is on-going and, in fact, becoming a worse degradation as each day passes. Teilhard de Chardin considered that it is through Christ that we glimpse the underlying spiritual element of Creation and that it is in humility and careful attention that we are granted the ability to see.

> *Through the mediation of Christ, the supernatural cosmos exposed its roots, closely woven into the universe. It was our world that the Saviour germinated: and he grows again and reaches his full stature through the continuation of our humble labours and our patience.*[27]

This is a very helpful reflection because not only do we become observers of the deeper realities of Creation by approaching the childlike appreciation of the learner, as far as we can, but the exposure of Christ in the midst of the natural world in all its

[27] Teilhard de Chardin, *The Hymn of the Universe*, p. 85.

creative energy grows – as we show humility and patience in its engagement. We bring this idea to birth in our attempts to support environmental protection and enhancement projects, and with a desire for a Christian intention in pressing on with campaigning for greater care for habitats and individual species, as well as protesting against the needless destruction and exploitation of nature through carelessness and greed.

PRAYER

Father,
grant us humility and patience
when we seem to possess little of either.
Lay your reviving hand
upon our fevered lives,
and bring to pass what you would have us do,
through Jesus Christ our Lord.
Amen.

DAY 16 (16th September)

An Awesome God

Isaiah 40:12

> *Who has measured the waters in the hollow of his hand and marked off the heavens with a span, enclosed the dust of the earth in a measure and weighed the mountains in scales and the hills in a balance?*

IF YESTERDAY WE considered the sight of the Almighty within the sight of the World, today it is imagining the colossal scale of God's greatness when weighed against the measure of all we physically know, at least on the planet on which we live. In fact, using the picture of a balance as part of the vision of this overwhelming power and influence, we are asked to consider the hills and mountains as objects to be weighed and compared on the scales. This is one of the Old Testament texts that most clearly makes this point, but there are others: examples of hills and forests, seas and huge beasts, deserts and even the stars in the heavens that exist only in the sway of the Lord.

A week ago, in the poetry of Job, we were drawn to feel small and inadequate, and to know our need in the face of the sweep of Nature's glory as imagined in a physical construction of

Heaven and Earth revealed in yesterday's psalm, whilst today, for the prophet Isaiah, the place of humanity is so diminished as to be like a grain of sand or a drop of water when compared to the Almighty power of God. Later in the chapter inhabitants of the earth are likened to grasshoppers. There are parallels, such as the one in last week's reading, in Job, and in Proverbs, in Genesis and elsewhere in Isaiah. But what does it all mean? Why is this chapter and the other texts similar to it across the Old Testament found in the Scriptures?

Specifically, chapter 40 of Isaiah ends with an appeal for waiting, not though in order to increase knowledge and learn from the humility of the careful observer. The reader is urged, after many verses of heightened awareness of God's influence in the world, that the weak and exhausted are to be lifted up on the wings of eagles, and to find new energy, and the ability to 'run and not be weary', to 'walk and not faint'.[28]

Many times have I read Isaiah 40 and I never fail to find in it reason to be hopeful and energised. Through the words of Job last week, we found a greater ability to see; through the words of Isaiah today we accept, and indeed, know, the strength to bring vision to reality. We shall rise up and be strong in the Lord, because he imparts such strength from the formidable resources of almighty power. It seems as though nothing is outside our ability to notice and be inspired, as the breath of a wind or the warmth of the sun or the light on rippling water reminds us of who put it there, or, as Teilhard de Chardin puts it beautifully:

---

[28] Isaiah 40:31.

> *A limpid sound arises amidst the silence; a trail of pure colour drifts through the glassy light glows for a moment in the depths of the eyes I love[...] Three things, tiny, fugitive: a song, a sunbeam, a glance.*[29]

We are in a Season of Creation, which is a time set aside by the Church, universally, in which there is an element of remembering – almost inevitably, as we consider significant change within a human lifespan. Consequently, we are not just looking at Creation, but may find ourselves considering how we order our lives, conscious of God's eternal perspective. Life may, in fact, take on a renewed fullness and joy that prompts, as simple and tenuous as a glance with fresh eyes, an impact so great that the wings of an eagle soaring in flight are but the pinions that carry us upwards, emotionally and spiritually. A feeling of youthfulness renewed and energy revived. 'We are not [...] simply nurselings rocked and suckled by mother earth'[30] but find ourselves raised by Christ to new realms of work and life. Isaiah's words in chapter 40 are to be read with the caution, 'beware, these verses can inspire change'. The prayer today is one by Teilhard de Chardin himself:

[29] Teilhard de Chardin, *The Hymn of the Universe*, p.109.
[30] Teilhard de Chardin, *The Hymn of the Universe*, p. 95.

PRAYER

Lord, that I might hold you more closely.
I would that my consciousness were as wide
    as the skies
and the earth and the peoples of the earth;
as deep as the past, the desert, the ocean;
as tenuous as the atoms of matter
or the thoughts of the human heart.[31]
Amen.

[31]   Teilhard de Chardin, *The Hymn of the Universe*, p. 117.

DAY 17 (17th September)

Lament

Joel 1:14-20

> *because the watercourses are dried up,*
> *and fire has devoured*
> *the pastures of the wilderness.*

THE DESTRUCTION OF habitat has become inevitable in virtually every area of the world today. Rising temperatures and sea levels, drought, floods, de-forestation, pollution, monoculture, opencast mining, over-population, war, de-regulation, ripping up of international agreements and protocols, have all, ultimately, contributed to degradation of the precious ecology of Nature. Whilst environmental campaigns frequently focus on one area or another, the wide-ranging causes of so much obliteration of God's Creation demonstrate that it is never one thing that is lost in isolation. The complicated web of Earth's ecosystems is groaning under the onslaught of uncontrolled human activity. All of this we know well, and this day is reserved as one of lament for what has been lost. Lament functions as an emotional release and is not directly linked to improved action, except through a changed attitude, from those whose blindness has been cured. Most lamentation is offered with open eyes; eyes that have led to the lament being sung, because of what they have seen clearly and unambiguously, as something bringing a welling up of tears and a wailing of voices in distress.

The book of the prophet Joel is heavy with lament, as the life of the Temple in Jerusalem responds to the issues of the day, and Joel, as part of the cult and liturgical practice, proclaims the need and provides the context for the people to lament at what is coming upon them. Through the lament Joel is expressing the pain of the nation, correcting its thinking and renewing its faith. Lament does not cause issues to vanish, nor provides a release from pain, but, as the Book of Joel proceeds, hope and trust in God and his purposes is rediscovered and the people are revived.

The Christian is living and working in the mix of human suffering and endeavour as are those of other faiths and none, and, as we read words of lament from perhaps two and a half millennia ago, so the refinement of our own reflection and effort may be paralleled. Teilhard de Chardin spoke of 'cherishing the hollowness as well as the fullness of life'.[32] We could put it another way by saying that we force ourselves to look at what we do not want to see, as we are drawn to what is attracting us, and by so doing we illuminate the whole scene, and apprehend what is happening in the shadows. To 'cherish' such looking means we are truly valuing what suffering teaches us, and that is a very sensitive area of transferred trauma, leaving us potentially less able, at least in the short term, to be prepared to take action. This suggests that lament is not a process for the individual, but to be embraced by a community of whatever scale, but not alone. Joel's experience is illustrating this point precisely at the centre of cultic and liturgical life in the Temple.

In Père Teilhard's work on the inner life *Le Milieu Divin*, he writes on the Christian's outlook on 'matter'. The scientific side of his nature is apparent in this objectivising of his approach

---

[32]   Teilhard de Chardin, *Le Milieu Divin*, p. 94.

to the investigation of what is our physical relationship with God's Creation. There is an indication that Teilhard may have believed in dualism with matter and spirit existing in separation, one physical and found in time and space and the other not so limited. However, there is more than enough of the investigative scientist about him, to ensure that a unity whereby matter and spirit interact is vital to him:

> *On the one hand matter is the burden, the fetters, the pain, the sin and the threat to our lives. It weighs us down, suffers, wounds, tempts and grows old. Matter makes us heavy, paralysed, vulnerable, guilty. Who will deliver us from this body of death?*
>
> *But at the same time matter is physical exuberance, enabling contact, virile effort and the joy of growth. It attracts, renews and unites and flowers. By matter we are nourished, lifted up, linked to everything else, invaded by life. To be deprived of it is intolerable.*[33]

So, the need to lament, and indeed the power of lamentation to affect our soul and the very heart of our life, is related to the way in which it holds the two sides of our physical nature in harmony, and yet in tension, as Teilhard de Chardin expresses it. The process of lamentation within a community is seen in the collective trauma of gatherings at the point of some personal or community event that damages an individual or family, either through internal or external attack, or as a result of natural disaster. An outpouring of grief, often with anger too, is experienced with

[33] Teilhard de Chardin, *Le Milieu Divin*, p.106.

the vow to seek to prevent a repetition. 'This must never happen again' is so often the cry, and frequently leads to funding and on-going support being found within that community to help this promise to be implemented.

PRAYER

Father,
may the lamentation of your people
come to your ears, and be fashioned
within our society to create a new resolve,
to prevent the repetition of
damage to lives and the environment
of which we are a part.
Bless those whose endeavours
draw their community to
desire not just the crying, in sorrow or anger
but to the promise of new ways
that will bring positive change,
to heal and rebuild for a sustainable future.
Through Jesus Christ we pray.
Amen.

DAY 18 (18th September)

Restitution

Joel 2:21-24

Do not fear, O soil;
be glad and rejoice,
for the Lord has done great things!

Do not fear, you animals of the field,
for the pastures of the wilderness are green;
the tree bears its fruit,
the fig tree and vine give their full yield.

O children of Zion, be glad
and rejoice in the Lord your God;
for he has given the early rain for your
*   vindication,*
he has poured down for you abundant rain,
the early and the later rain, as before.
The threshing floors shall be full of grain,
the vats shall overflow with wine and oil.

JOEL IS WRITING with the hope of the end of affliction and suffering. This state of mind is common to all humanity and to every era of human life. Living under constant threat, with little or nothing of the necessities of life and facing death every day, and that of the vulnerable, the children and elderly especially, remains the crying shame of our so-called civilised world. One needs hardly record the centres of conflict in the twenty-first century, they are already in your minds as you read this, and lie heavy on your hearts, as they do on mine. The prophet paints his own picture, and it is of restoration of the whole environment, not simply a saving of a people through convoys of aid, such as has been the case from the famine in Joseph's time that drove his brothers to seek grain in Egypt, to today's under-funded international aid.

Water has appeared on quite a number of the days of this Creation Season reflection, and appears again from Joel today. Part of the promise, of the dream, of the hope is for the 'early rain' – a sign of a vindicated people, then abundant rain, not just the early rain, but the later rain will not fail either. The outcome is 'threshing floors [...] full of grain, the vats overflow[ing] with wine and oil'. Simone Weil wrote on affliction and love and would have understood the Joel transition from the hopelessness of the people's rejection of God and the disaster they encountered, but she identifies the core reason for that disaster is not offence given to God, but the wrong choices made by the people, leading to their own demise. Sense eventually prevails and the land is restored, but the pain and suffering are not forgotten – for a while, anyway ...

> *One can only accept the existence of affliction by considering it at a distance.*
> *God created through love and for love, God did not create anything except love itself, and the means to love. He created love in all its forms.*

He created beings capable of love from all possible distances. Because no other could do it, he himself went to the greatest possible distance, the infinite distance. This infinite distance between God and God, this supreme tearing apart, this agony beyond all others, this marvel of love, is the crucifixion. Nothing can be further from God than that which has been made accursed.

This tearing apart, over which supreme love places the bond of supreme union, echoes perpetually across the universe in the midst of the silence, like two notes, separate yet melting into one, like pure and heart-rending harmony. This is the Word of God. The whole creation is nothing but its vibration.[34]

Before we settle ourselves to contemplate how a nation, or a community within a nation, recovers from affliction, and by extension think about how nature may recover from an onslaught on its systems and structure, such as continues to occur, the same metaphors can be applied. Simone Weil gives the example of the hammer and nail, which gives a particularly brutal picture of the damage caused in both cases:

When we hit a nail with a hammer, the whole shock received by the large head of the nail passes into the point without any of it being lost, although it is only a point. If the hammer and the head of the nail were infinitely big it would be just the same. The point of the nail would transmit this infinite shock at the point to which it was applied.

[34] Simone Weil, *Waiting on God*, p. 68.

> *Extreme affliction, which means physical pain, distress of soul and social degradation, all at the same time, constitutes the nail. The point is applied at the very centre of the soul.*[35]

'The earth is the Lord's and all that is in it', is what we say often enough echoing the Scriptures, but resonating with our thoughts of how we experience nature. I recall once on retreat being encouraged to walk the paths of a beautiful example of Hampshire countryside, along a chalk stream, through woods and over heath. After some time, a couple of hours, I think, we were to bring back something that meant something to us and would be a reflection on our state of mind or heart at that moment. Most of us did the obvious thing and stole a flower, a bottle of water from the crystal clear stream, a leaf or even a stone. In my memory there was a single object that struck us all and that was a large branch fallen from a tree, that one cleric lugged back. I am not sure why, these years later, but I imagine it was to do with the burden of what has fallen and lies before one, inescapable and unavoidable. That is our afflicted world, and if Simone Weil is right, and I believe she is, the distance between what we are experiencing in the tragedy and crying agony of the destruction of so much that we hold precious and the loving God, whom we appeal to daily in prayer, is about as wide as from the manger to the cross.

[35]   Simone Weil, *Waiting on God*, p. 77.

PRAYER

Creator God,
fill our souls with the desire
for each other in compassion and love,
and may that human bond
be reflected as we touch
every element of your nature,
much that we cannot see or know,
but in the world around us
let us see your glory
and respect it as from your hand.
In blessing may we be blessed,
and share that blessing in the grace
of Christ our Lord.
Amen.

DAY 19 (19th September)

Where does Wisdom Lie?

Ecclesiasticus 51:3-16

> *While I was still young,*
> *I sought Wisdom openly in my prayer.*
> *Before the temple I asked for her,*
> *and I will search for her until the end.*
> *From the first blossom to the ripening grape,*
> *my heart delighted in her.*
> *My foot walked on the straight path,*
> *from my youth I followed her steps.*
> *I inclined my ear and received her,*
> *I found for myself much instruction.*

IN JUNE 2010 I was with a group of clergy at Minsteracres Retreat Centre in Northumberland. During our time there we were led by Andrew John, until 2025 Archbishop of Wales, but before his elevation, when he was simply Bishop of Bangor. I was reminded of this when reading of St Asaph, whose life is celebrated on 5 May, and dwelling on the distances travelled and the connections made across the country. I was thinking, as I chanced to find my notes of a decade and a half ago, and I was pondering the depth of teaching that Bishop Andy gave us during those days, when we were immersed in the Northumbrian

Church and visited Lindisfarne, amongst other places.

One morning the bishop asked us to undertake an interesting exercise, which it would be worth attempting again today. He asked us to list the top ten words indicating the 'language of spirituality' in today's Church. If I recall correctly, he didn't unpack exactly what he meant by 'the language of spirituality', he simply gave us an example, by asking 'Would "humility" feature in the top ten?' Good question I felt then. Good question I feel now. As we were turning this over in our minds, and probably considering the coffee break that was imminent, he told us of the thought he had, on the day of his consecration as bishop, to once a week clean the floor of his chapel on his hands and knees, as a private act of humility.

So why did he tell us this? At first sight it may appear as just the opposite of what he was teaching us, as if he were seeking praise for his act and vow. The way he told it quickly dismissed any thought of such an idea. The example was a good one and we took it to heart. I even made a note of it, and the subsequent teaching, to read much later, for what he went on to tell us wasn't 'How to live humbly' but, 'What is the effect upon our lives if we do not embrace humility?' By putting it this way, his action was not something out of the way and unusual. He was simply giving us a mindset that should be our norm as Christians, and particularly as clergy.

His angle of attack at our pride was incisive: 'Humility saves us from the great temptation in seeking popularity.' He went on relentlessly at this point: 'If we find that we are in a conflict situation in our ministry we will take any affirmation that comes our way. But, humility saves us from resting our service on popularity and success.'

Then, taking the example of the hymn 'Brother, sister, let me serve you', he drew us to consider the post-resurrection lakeside encounter between Peter and Jesus. Bishop Andy pointed out to us that 'Jesus was taking a risk in asking Peter to take risks.' But that this was the only way for him, and for us too, if we are not to shut-down the working of grace within us. 'If we can't be wounded, we are of no use to anyone. We need to incarnate in our lives the knocks and bruises.'

It is strange how we are forever re-learning lessons as we seek Wisdom (and I capitalise the word, to give it the meaning from Ecclesiasticus above) – how we need to be forever re-learning lessons ('*I will search for her until the end*'). Retreats function in this way, allowing time for recollection and reflection. We rarely discover anything entirely new, but the ground is broken up and the rigidity of the filters and lenses through which we look at ourselves and the world – and perhaps God too – is weakened. We start to look at those filters and lenses, and allow them to withdraw like mist burning off on a day in summer.

That day in Northumberland it rained. The lake was bordered with yellow flag iris, the hawthorn blossom was still not at its best, the tiny stamens like stars in each flower, the birds flitting from damp bush to damp bush, and there was a great calm.

> *I inclined my ear and received her,*
> *I found for myself much instruction.*

This, indeed, is the *softer* side of the understanding of Wisdom, if I might use a word that I suspect is grossly inadequate. When Simone Weil spoke of affliction in a quotation yesterday she saw herself as the justifiable recipient of such affliction from a loving God whose discipline is both necessary and desirable.

I never read the story of the barren fig tree without trembling. I think that it is a portrait of me. In it also, nature was powerless, and yet it was not excused. Christ cursed it.

> *That is why although there are perhaps not any particular faults in my life which are really serious [...] I think when I consider things in the cold light of reason that I have more just cause to fear God's anger than many a great criminal.*
>
> *It is not that I actually do fear it. By a strange twist, the thought of God's anger only arouses love in me. It is the thought of the possible favour of God and of his mercy that makes me tremble with a sort of fear.*
>
> *On the other hand the sense of being like a barren fig tree for Christ tears my heart.*[36]

In our day, looking from the first blossom to the ripening grape, or any other sequence of growth from start to finish, is a wholesome, a patient, process of seeking to understand the natural life that encompasses us everyday, and is especially obvious in spring and summer. From the perspective of a gardener there is ever the feeling of living in some kind of symbiotic union with the plants, as we grow together for mutual

---

[36] Simone Weil, *Waiting on God*, p. 47.

benefit. The breakdown of Wisdom's capacity to enrich and encourage the stirring of faith, which occurs in the observation of the barren fig tree, leaves us in no doubt as to the need to stay alert at all times and work for the sake of others.

PRAYER

Lord God Almighty,
through observing the fruitfulness
of your Creation,
we can see too the Wisdom
in which it is made and sustained.
Grant that we may strive to be the fruitful
    vine
rather than the barren fig tree,
in your sight and for your world.
Amen.

DAY 20 (20th September)

The Universality of Love

The Song of Three

O ye light and darkness, bless ye the Lord: praise and exalt him above all for ever.
O ye ice and cold, bless ye the Lord: praise and exalt him above all for ever.
O ye frost and snow, bless ye the Lord: praise and exalt him above all for ever.
O ye lightnings and clouds, bless ye the Lord: praise and exalt him above all for ever.
O let the earth bless the Lord: praise and exalt him above all for ever.
O ye mountains and little hills, bless ye the Lord: praise and exalt him above all for ever.
O all ye things that grow in the earth, bless ye the Lord: praise and exalt him above all for ever.
O ye mountains, bless ye the Lord: Praise and exalt him above all for ever.
O ye seas and rivers, bless ye the Lord: praise and exalt him above all for ever.
O ye whales, and all that move in the waters, bless ye the Lord: praise and exalt him above all for ever.
O all ye fowls of the air, bless ye the Lord: praise and exalt him above all for ever.
O all ye beasts and cattle, bless ye the Lord: praise and exalt him above all for ever.
O ye children of men, bless ye the Lord: praise and exalt him above all for ever.

THERE IS SOMETHING in the Benedicite that speaks to me not just of praise, but of freedom; of a breath of fresh air in a stale and tired world. I couldn't leave this book without at least part of what the three men in the furnace lived through as they praised God, imagining that the whole world was doing that too. The world of today is looking at increased temperatures in air and sea already taking effect, but likely to become more pronounced as the decades of this century unfold. We know this to be patchy, with some areas experiencing other extremes of weather, but overall the picture is of melting glaciers, warming seas, and in places that are already warm and dry, the expectation is for more heat and even less rain. One of the major dangers is that countries and peoples will become more and more protective of their resources and potentially wars will be fought over scarce commodities, minerals, and perhaps most of all, water.

Writing in a letter dated 26 May 1942, more than eighty years ago, Simone Weil stated:

> *We are living in times which have no precedent, and in our present situation universality, which could formerly be implicit, has to be fully explicit. It has to permeate our language and the whole of our way of life.*[37]

Protectionism is a feature of our day, and attachment to the institutions of society, as much as to the nation itself, at the expense of a universal concern for the world, its entire population and its complex ecology, is indeed becoming the normally accepted pattern of human behaviour. One can give 'explicit' examples to disprove the general trend, and many NGOs pride themselves on their universality and inclusive approach, often working in extremely difficult and dangerous situations.

[37] Simone Weil, *Waiting on God*, p. 45.

> *It is true that we have to love our neighbour, but, in the example that Christ gave as an illustration of this commandment, the neighbour is a being of whom nothing is known, lying naked, bleeding and unconscious on the road. It is a question of completely anonymous, and for that reason completely universal love.*[38]

The Song of Three is linked to a specific event and a specific period in Israel's history. One in which exile and suppression were being borne with prayer, stoicism and faith by a relatively small band of remarkable servants of Yahweh. But it is the breadth of acknowledgement of the Divine praise that is astounding; every creature, and even the inanimate particles of Creation sing out their praise to God most high. To save the planet in these days of climate crisis, there is a place for seeing the praise of the very things in our sight that may be being affected by that crisis, as confirming the need for all humanity to put to one side the narrow concerns of those who place our day above the future, and the health of their country before the needs of the world.

> *The children of God should not have any other country here below but the universe itself, with the totality of all the reasoning creatures it ever has contained, contains, or ever will contain. That is the native city to which we owe our love.*[39]

[38] Simone Weil, *Waiting on God*, p. 45.
[39] Simone Weil, *Waiting on God*, p. 44.

PRAYER

O heavenly and universal King,
Lord of lords and loving Father,
we confess our need to look wider,
and deeper and more honestly
at the elements of Creation that praise
and magnify and glorify your name.
Make us wary of the lesser loyalties
of this life, while hiding from others
the universal love of Nature,
through Christ your Son our Lord.
Amen.

DAY 21 (21st September)

Do Not Be Anxious

Matthew 6:26-29

> *Look at the birds of the air; they neither sow nor reap nor gather into barns, and yet your heavenly Father feeds them. Are you not of more value than they? And can any of you by worrying add a single hour to your span of life? And why do you worry about clothing? Consider the lilies of the field, how they grow; they neither toil nor spin, yet I tell you, even Solomon in all his glory was not clothed like one of these.*

THE MYSTERY THAT is the placing of life, freedom and permanence together, though ultimately that is not for every individual organism and every person, but collectively, is in the providence of God's loving nature. The ability to release one's grip upon what is held in trust, unto life itself, is one that Jesus said was life-giving. It is a discovery too deep for words, but lying in the heart of the mind that has found true love, true life and true hope. This mystery is not static either. We are part, should we choose to be, of a spiritual household that recognises that the power of the second of the great commandments, that we love our neighbour as ourself, is immense.

As the Samaritan on the road to Jericho lifted a wounded member of the race that despised him onto his own donkey, with wounds bound and life and hope restored, the miracle of reconciliation met the miracle of love. It was a moment that Jesus declared in story-form, but which has gained reality over and over again in numerous examples of giving in compassion and out of a heart tuned to no other way. When viewing the future of the human race, Teilhard de Chardin came to the conclusion that the only way for humanity to continue to survive and flourish was to create an environment that would provide hope for all peoples, regardless of their background and situation. As he saw it, such would be:

> *a special and novel environment [which] has been evolved among human individuals within which they acquire the faculty of associating together, and reacting upon one another, no longer primarily for the preservation and continuance of the species but for the creation of a common consciousness.*[40]

Although not published until 1959, *The Future of Man* was written over the course of thirty years, from shortly after the First World War until after the Second World War. This backdrop to his vision of humanity's future is one that insists that the human species has not simply evolved physically and even mentally, but in an inner capacity to be increasingly spiritually attuned, an element of which is the closer attention to one another. This 'socialisation' as he described it is beyond 'the massing together of individualities

---

[40]   Teilhard de Chardin, *The Future of Man*, p. 54.

[…] but a 'conspiracy' informed with love […] it is the fundamental impulse of Life, or if you prefer, the one natural medium in which the rising course of evolution can proceed.'[41]

> *With love omitted there is truly nothing ahead of us except the forbidding prospect of standardisation and enslavement […] It is through love and within love that we must look for the deepening of our deepest self, in the life-giving coming together of humankind.*[42]

The passage from the Sermon on the Mount taken as today's reading is most obviously concerned with freeing us from anxiety, but it indicates within this very teaching that what springs from a loving God can encourage our evolution, through observation, and the gradual acquiring of the lesson that that observation is in itself the means to evolve spiritually, towards a more complete understanding of the authorship of the very life that flickers like a swallow before our eyes, or waves in the breeze like meadow grasses and the wildflowers that grow within them.

> *Love is the free and imaginative outpouring of the spirit over all unexplored paths. It links those who love in bonds that unite but do not confound, causing them to discover in their mutual contact an exaltation capable, incomparably more than any arrogance of solitude, of arousing the heart of their being all that they possess of uniqueness and creative power.*[43]

[41] Teilhard de Chardin, *The Future of Man*, p. 54.
[42] Teilhard de Chardin, *The Future of Man*, pp. 54, 55.
[43] Teilhard de Chardin, *The Future of Man*, p. 55.

The capacity for love outpoured to be a creative power is, if for nothing else besides, a perfect antidote for individuals who have become frozen into inactivity and hopelessness. Anxiety may evaporate, and the very sight of something ephemeral may restore hope in the eternal.

PRAYER

Lord Jesus,
you taught your followers to
look to the passing things of Nature,
and consider God's love for them,
drawing a parallel with our fear
of losing the necessities of life.
May we take the opportunity,
often and at leisure,
to value the gift of sight,
and proclaim the miracle of life,
in the world around us.
Amen.

DAY 22 (22nd September)

Jesus, Reflecting God's Glory

Hebrews 1:1-3

> *Long ago God spoke to our ancestors in many and various ways by the prophets, but in these last days he has spoken to us by a Son, whom he appointed heir of all things, through whom he also created the worlds. He is the reflection of God's glory and the exact imprint of God's very being, and he sustains all things by his powerful word. When he had made purification for sins, he sat down at the right hand of the Majesty on high [...]*

I RECALL AN occasion when for no particular reason the Epistle to the Hebrews popped up for me twice in a day. Not amidst the lectionary readings but from two books that I was dipping into. The first was by way of a throwback to the 1970s when, as I was studying for a primary degree in Divinity, there appeared the Paternoster Church History series, with such engaging titles as *The Spreading Flame, The Growing Storm, The Morning Star, The Great Light, Light in the North* and *The Inextinguishable Blaze*. How could one not be inspired by the history of the Church through these readable volumes!

F. F. Bruce, primarily a biblical scholar, producing commentaries and numerous other works, wrote the first volume on the early Church, entitled *The Spreading Flame.* I had always meant to read it, but never did. I acquired a copy a short while ago, and it has been looking down at me from a high shelf since then. It starts in Corinth, diving straight in, as one of the important early churches faced with all kinds of potential and real challenges, both within and beyond the Church fellowship, seeks under the guidance of Paul and others to establish its life and witness in what was quite a hub of first-century life.

Through reference to the Acts of the Apostles, the Pauline Epistles and other non-canonical texts, Bruce reports on how things developed, as the threats and persecution, as well as the growth and internal conflict in the church are examined, He then, almost in passing, introduces the Epistle to the Hebrews in this interesting way as the early believers in Jesus wondered why, through all the turmoil, Jesus had not yet returned:

> *[a] group of Jewish Christians received a communication from a friend whose name has been forgotten [...] he wrote to steady those who were wavering and imbue them with the necessary patience. Did the coming of Jesus seem deferred? Let them cheer up; yet a little while and the Coming One will come and make no delay[...]*[44]

Later, I had my second reminder of Hebrews, reading one of Ronald Blythe's thoughtful

[44] F. F. Bruce, *The Spreading Flame* (The Paternoster Press, 1958), p.152, The reference is to Hebrews 10:37.

reflections from *Stour Seasons* (2016) in which he quotes the author of Hebrews referring to Christ as 'the effulgence of God's glory' and our high priest. He does so in connection with John Bunyan, who, believing that he had committed an unforgivable sin, listened to his wife who read him these calming words from Hebrews:

> *Remember where you stand, not before the palpable blazing fire of Sinai, with the darkness, gloom and whirlwind, the trumpet blast and the oracular voice […] No, you stand before the city of the living God, heavenly Jerusalem […] the spirits of good men made perfect, and Jesus the mediator of a new covenant, whose sprinkled blood has better things to tell than the blood of Abel.*[45]

As Christians throughout the ages have been steadied in their faith through the reading of the Epistle to the Hebrews and other parts of the Scriptures, so we learn from their struggles and their patient faith in times of our own pilgrimage. Patience, patience; what a need we all have of this Christian quality – one of the fruits of a Spirit-filled life listed by St Paul writing to the Galatians: love, joy, peace, patience, kindness, goodness, faithfulness, gentleness, and self-control.

[45]   R. Blythe, *Stour Seasons* (Canterbury Press, 2016), p. 37.

PRAYER

God of our ancestors, and God of today,
remind us of all that your glory reveals,
and bring us in humility to consider
the very Creation that reflects your heart of
    love.
In Christ your Son, our Lord and Saviour,
we commit to greater care for the World in
    which we live.
Help us to see ways, each day, to restore and
    revitalise
what we have so often abused and destroyed.
This we pray in Jesus' name.
Amen.

DAY 23 (23rd September)

Peace – Be Still

Mark 4:35-41

On that day, when evening had come, he said to them, 'Let us go across to the other side.' And leaving the crowd behind, they took him with them in the boat, just as he was. Other boats were with him. A great windstorm arose, and the waves beat into the boat, so that the boat was already being swamped. But he was in the stern, asleep on the cushion; and they woke him up and said to him, 'Teacher, do you not care that we are perishing?' He woke up and rebuked the wind, and said to the sea, 'Peace! Be still!' Then the wind ceased, and there was a dead calm. He said to them, 'Why are you afraid? Have you still no faith?' And they were filled with great awe and said to one another, 'Who then is this, that even the wind and the sea obey him?'

THERE IS MORE than one example of misunderstanding between the disciples and Jesus in the four Gospels. In some cases, such as when our Lord spoke of his impending suffering, it was disbelief tinged with a very real fear of what that meant for them all. On another occasion, the followers of Jesus were discussing who was the greatest, a question which echoes down the centuries, and is not unknown in our day, as are the feelings of being slighted and looking for revenge. In the story of the stilling of the storm, however, we have a gut reaction to a storm that threatened to swamp the boat. They were terrified, and Jesus seemed to be sleeping peacefully through it all. Their level of anxiety climaxed at the point of waking him, and crying for help.

Jesus, in rebuking the wind and calming the sea, demonstrates that his power can be impersonal, as well as loving and healing and accepting of his fellow beings. This story does present a quite different picture to that with which we are perhaps more familiar. We recognise that our Lord had the power to upset the natural laws, and to call for peace and calm where they were not to be found, The story shows just how necessary it is that we do not take too cosy a picture of the transcendence of God and the cosmic relevance of Christ, through whom all things were brought into being. The paradox with the one who walks with us and engages with our innermost thoughts, and empathises with a single individual, is one we learn to live with rather than comprehend, across the billions of human lives and the complexity of an ecological mystery that binds all life within the scope of the Father's loving concern.

This aspect of our relationship with our Lord, as being both deeply personal and, at the same time, able to be conceived with an impersonal and distant aspect, recognising the gulf that separates us, as well as the love which unites us, may also be true of the interface between human endeavour and the natural world. Ruination of one's personal landscape is fought energetically and with strong advocacy for the species at risk, be they birds, butterflies, plants, mammals or insects, but the wrecking of the planet as a whole, and worsening conditions for those thousands of miles away is less likely to be opposed with the same degree of passion.

Simone Weil suggests that *renunciation* is the binding principle of humanity that allows impersonal feelings (that blunt our effectiveness and extenuate the distance between ourselves and the concern for the lives of others) to become transformed through sensitive and compassionate engagement. At least, I believe that to be her intention, in demonstrating that through obedience to God and the divine example of Jesus Christ, possessing, as we do, the free will to offer ourselves in this way, there is created within us a capacity of letting go, of release, to the point of the acceptance of our own suffering and affliction, because it is a renunciation that is grounded in love. The principle of allowing all human beings the right of possessing freedom to be able to make this act of renunciation, also insists that every human being treats every other human being as being gifted with the dignity of personality – unique and precious – and that the only rights one may possess and may claim are those one can grant equally to any other.

We are made in the very image of God. It is by virtue of something in us which attaches to the fact of being a person but which is not the fact itself. It is the power of renouncing our own personality. It is obedience.

[...]

It is because the renunciation of the personality makes man a reflection of God that it is so frightful to reduce men to the condition of inert matter by plunging them into affliction. When the quality of human personality is taken from them, the possibility of renouncing it is also taken away, except in the case of those who are sufficiently prepared. As God has created our independence so that we should have the possibility of renouncing it out of love, we should for the same reason wish to preserve the independence of our fellows. He who is perfectly obedient sets an infinite price upon the faculty of free choice in all men.[46]

The domination of whole peoples and nations, whether by internal dictatorship or external control, eliminates the possibility of free will being expressed without the significant risk of imprisonment, torture, psychological and physical, and often leading to disappearance, unending incarceration and death. Yet how is this seen and experienced in the light of our Lord's miracle of the stilling of the storm. Has it, in fact, any relevance? The action of humanity in ecologically changing aspects of the world is sometimes declared to be it 'playing God'. Increasingly over the past few decades the environmental damage inflicted upon our planet has been known to be deliberate and arrogant. If humanity were able to reverse any of this by the waving of a magic wand, and thereby still its

[46] Simone Weil, *Waiting on God*, pp. 114, 115.

own storm of destruction and fear, then such an impersonal action, in so far as it restores freedom to at least some people on Earth, becomes a personal action of the re-creation of free will, in a world that restricts this very gift to so many.

PRAYER

Father,
grant us the eyes to see,
and the heart to understand,
how many are denied free will
and the chance to find
their own path of self-determination.
Bless all who seek to re-establish
true equity amongst your people,
and in your whole Creation
in Jesus Christ, your Son,
our Lord.
Amen.

DAY 24 (24th September)

The Sower

Luke 8:4-8

> *When a great crowd gathered and people from town after town came to him, he said in a parable: 'A sower went out to sow his seed; and as he sowed, some fell on the path and was trampled on, and the birds of the air ate it up. Some fell on the rock; and as it grew up, it withered for lack of moisture. Some fell among thorns, and the thorns grew with it and choked it. Some fell into good soil, and when it grew, it produced a hundredfold.' As he said this, he called out, 'Let anyone with ears to hear listen!'*

THE PARABLE THAT Jesus tells, to indicate whether or not the Word of God will take root in the human heart, is based upon the physical rooting of seedlings of grain cast on the soil in Palestine. The twin dangers of being dried up or choked are apparent, and the story is graphically told, with the birds taking their opportunity to feed when they could. Being blessed with rain was assumed. Going on pilgrimage to the Holy Land on a number of occasions, I generally planned to time it for the springtime when the hills of Galilee were clothed in waving grasses and wild flowers, having benefitted from the rainfall during the November to April period. Once the summer arrives, the fields turn to straw and the baked soil is dried up in the sun. Irrigating the fields of crops from limited resources, drawing increasingly from the river Jordan and the Sea of Galilee, has left just a trickle arriving in the Dead Sea, which is much reduced in size and divided into two lakes with a narrow channel between them.

Today, there are many places with a far greater natural problem with water, or, at least, the lack of it. Historically, already very warm areas of the world are losing much of their expected annual rainfall. This has happened in places as far apart as areas of Spain, Australia and North Africa. Generally speaking tropical areas are anticipating more rain, and sub-tropical areas – such as around the Mediterranean Sea – are becoming drier. Whilst we are not needing to re-tell the Parable of the Sower for the twenty-first century, if anything it is an even more pertinent example as the good soil is the moisture retentive ground for the seed. Seed cast on other ground have no chance, and even the temporary flourish would be retarded.

The parable aside, referring as it does to the individual response to the Word of God taking root or otherwise in the human heart, its lesson from nature has a contemporary relevance to Christians looking at what is happening from a perception of Creation as a divine activity, and to all humanity searching for an adequate response. Teilhard de Chardin, writing after living through the two World Wars of the twentieth century, commented passionately about what he termed *The Planetisation of Mankind*, the moving together of all peoples and within the mix the consequences that were appearing:

> *[…] since 1939 […] during these six years, despite the unleashing of so much hatred, the human block has not disintegrated. On the contrary, in its most rigid organic depths it has further increased its vice-like grip upon us all. First 1914-1918, then 1939-1945 – two successive turns of the screw. Every new war, embarked upon by the nations for the purpose of detaching themselves from one another, merely results in them being bound and mingled together in a more inextricable knot. The more we seek to thrust away, the more do we interpenetrate.*
>
> *Indeed, how could it be otherwise?*[47]

Pierre Teilhard shares his thoughts as to the wisdom and life, or otherwise, which emanates from what he describes as, 'the vast and pitiless confusion of peoples, […] [with] whole armies being removed from one hemisphere to another, and tens of thousands of refugees being scattered across the world like seed borne on the wind.'[48] Eighty years on and the tide of human activity has led to a greater understanding of the damage inflicted upon the planet, and the real cost to many people, with millions having been denied the life they should have had. Teilhard paints some depressing pictures, then ends the section with the words:

[47]   Teilhard de Chardin, *The Future of Man*, pp. 126, 127.
[48]   Teilhard de Chardin, *The Future of Man*, p. 126.

Let us look it in the face and see whether, using it as an unassailable foundation, we cannot erect upon it a hopeful edifice of joy and liberation.[49]

Emerging from the darkness, as was the world when he wrote these words, let us take heart and find the joy and liberation through concerted effort for the sake of all peoples of the world, and for the health of the planet upon which we all live.

PRAYER

Father,
as we hear your Word,
may we be as the good ground,
listening and growing in our faith.
Help us to look at the world
with eyes of hope,
and by our prayers and our action,
bring hope to others.
That the world may rejoice,
and all Creation sing your praise.
In Christ Jesus, our Lord.
Amen.

[49] Teilhard de Chardin, *The Future of Man*, p. 128.

DAY 25 (25th September)

The Vine

John 15:5

THE BIBLE IS full of references to the natural world, and Jesus was constantly drawing his allusions from the countryside. This not only links us into the flow of the life of Christ, as in the vine with many branches, it establishes us within the general flow of Nature. We abide in Christ, we also have a sense of abiding as part of the divine Creation. I have a particular attraction to six words of Pierre Teilhard that he uses more than once, and I have found myself dwelling on these words, and different aspects of their meaning – not all those meanings are their author's, I am quite certain. The six words are:

Man came silently into the world[50]

Teilhard de Chardin meant by this that there was, in his view, no cataclysmic activity that heralded

[50] Teilhard de Chardin, *The Phenomenon of Man*, p. 184, 186.

humanity's arrival. Whatever act of God produced human beings in the evolutionary path it was a quiet process of development occurring across the face of more than one area of the earth.

> *Man came silently into the world. As a matter of fact he trod so softly that, when we first catch sight of him as revealed by those indestructible stone instruments, we find him sprawling all over the old world from the Cape of Good Hope to Peking.*[51]

We are weighing contrasts, both in the branches of the vine that either bear fruit or not, and in the actions of the human race that are silently developing or silently destructive. Silence can indeed indicate humility and care, a hidden work of extraordinary importance that is simply not talked about, or it can indicate just the opposite: carelessness, actions hidden because they are life-denying, arrogance masquerading as support, whilst quietly dominating a situation with contempt.

Protests across the whole range of issues that inflame public opinion are vocal and visible or are pointless. Questioning the tactics of protesters has been an issue of its own in recent years. Can damage to a work of art, or bringing a motorway to a standstill, or ruining a concert or exhibition that people have spent a great deal of precious time and money attending, be acceptable? Alternatively, can denying protesters freedom of action that is not criminal but is disruptive, and perhaps quite costly, be allowed? There are fine lines to be drawn and freedoms to maintain,

---

[51] Teilhard de Chardin, *The Phenomenon of Man,* p. 186.

whilst protecting the common rights of the general public as well.

Jesus, in describing himself as a vine, is painting part of the picture of his place within the Kingdom that sees him as Shepherd, and the Way and the Truth and the Life, as well as a powerful image of Christ as the Light of the World. As all of these, and other descriptions mount up, so do the contrasts between what is of Christ and what is not. He himself declared that who is not with him is against him. In this complex mix of metaphors we find ourselves needing to respond. Our Lord expects this of us, as he expected it of his disciples in their day. In a way, a combining thread of all these images, physically or physiologically, is the fact of Life itself. As branches of a vine, we only have life while attached; as sheep we are lost, and risk losing our way and our life without the shepherd. The Way is life-defining, the Truth is life-asserting, and Christ's Life is the source of ours. Life on Earth requires Light, as we need the inner light to live eternally, and that light is Christ.

My musings on the idea of the 'silence' with which human life has come into this world, whilst accepting Teilhard's reasoning which produced the words he did, leads me to wonder about awe, and those moments when time stands still, when the human mind seeks to comprehend the miracle of what is happening – the realisation that one is witnessing something incredible and unrepeatable and amazing – and one cannot move, dare not move, in case through doing so the moment is marred.

I wonder how the disciples felt at the Last Supper when Jesus was telling them so many things and symbolically leaving them examples to follow, whilst sharing in the ordinary things of fellowship and friendship? Being bound to Christ even in the face of confusion, threat and death, as a branch, is part of the plant that has given it life, suggests that there could have been a few moments of silence and awe at that meal. I like to think so.

PRAYER

Lord Jesus,
may the branches of your vine
prove fruitful and full of life and vigour,
with joy and the shout of Alleluia,
may our lives ever be bound with yours!
In love....
Amen.

DAY 26 (26th September)

Eternal Power and Divine Nature

Romans 1:20

Ever since the creation of the world God's eternal power and divine nature, invisible though they are, have been seen and understood through the things God has made.

THE NATURAL WORLD, which is a constant for all peoples on Earth, though those in rural areas experience it more fully than others, remains a window onto God. The relationship of our appreciation of beauty and our love for God is a close one, and having written at length on the Old Testament book the Song of Songs[52], I am acutely aware of how the sight of beauty has been used to help us understand both desire and inner wellbeing, in relation to a constant knowledge and awareness of the divine presence. Just how easy this is inclined to tip over into sentimentality and misunderstanding of the nature of God is something that we are wary of avoiding, but nonetheless, those dangers exist, at the same time as allowing the

[52] John Mann, *Moments of Love* (Darton, Longman and Todd, 2025).

freedom of expression that the Song of Songs suggests to us, to fill our hearts with joy and love.

Simone Weil links the beauty of the world with compassion, which is not disconnected from this thought either:

> *[…] there is no contradiction between the love of the beauty of the world and compassion. Such love does not prevent us from suffering on our own account when we are in affliction. Neither does it prevent us from suffering because others are afflicted. It is on another plane from suffering.*
>
> *The love of the beauty of the world, while it is universal, involves, as a love which is secondary and subordinate to itself, the love of all the truly precious things which bad fortune can destroy. The truly precious things are those which form ladders reaching towards the beauty of the world, openings on to it. He who has gone farther, to the very beauty of the world itself, does not love them any less but much more deeply than before.*
>
> *Numbered among them are the pure and authentic achievements of art and science. In a much more general way they include everything which envelops human life with poetry through all the social strata. Every human being has at his roots here below a certain terrestrial poetry, a reflection of the heavenly glory, the link, of which he is more or less vaguely conscious, with his universal country. Affliction is the tearing up of these roots.*[53]

[53] Simone Weil, *Waiting on God*, p. 115.

Simone Weil is drawing us to a deeper place than enjoying a peaceful and glorious sunset, or basking in sunshine in a flower-filled meadow, or standing on top of a mountain and viewing the world below. She bids us look beneath to the way that we are rooted in the created world, because it reflects our own origins, and spiritually encompasses Heaven and Earth. The fact that affliction tears at these roots is not surprising, for it channels our attention below the superficial to the depths of our being, naked before God and knowing that in the region of that bare existence there is exposed the place of universal equality, love and eternal light, uncreated, both human and divine.

As St Paul indicates, the power and nature of God is invisible, but may be *seen* and *understood* through Creation. This suggests that Simone Weil is correct in connecting the ability we possess, through the experience of love, to fathom something of the way that God works in the world through what is visible to us – and that includes compassion and the experience of affliction. We may learn more than we realise through these deeply rendered characteristics of the divine/human interface. We shall not always succeed in understanding – I don't think Paul would claim that they are crystal clear – but the invisible and unfathomable may be pondered through what we can see, and that this will lead to some degree of understanding.

PRAYER

Father,
as we look,
with as searching eyes as we are able,
reveal to us
something of your power and nature.
May we grow in grace and understanding,
and, through both compassion and affliction,
recognise the depth of your love for all
      humanity.
In Jesus Christ we pray.
Amen.

DAY 27 (27th September)

Christ – Firstborn of All Creation

Colossians 1:15-17

> *He is the image of the invisible God, the firstborn of all creation, for in him all things in heaven and on earth were created, things visible and invisible, whether thrones or dominions or rulers or powers – all things have been created through him and for him. He himself is before all things, and in him all things hold together.*

IN THE BOOK *Teilhard de Chardin and the Mystery of Christ*, the American Jesuit academic Fr Christopher F. Mooney, drawing on his doctoral thesis, assembled the thoughts of Pierre Teilhard concerning Christ's revelation of the mystery of God and of the meaning of humanity, and 'therefore the ultimate meaning of that evolutionary process of which God is the cause and man the culmination.'[54]

It is through evolution that he eventually attained certitude on the natural level through his 'law of complexity-consciousness', his placing of man at the

[54] Christopher F. Mooney, *Teilhard de Chardin and the Mystery of Christ*, p. 5.

> *summit of the evolutionary process and his insistence that the cosmos is held together by spirit not matter, and converges towards persons not things.*[55]

Pierre Teilhard believed through this law of complexity-consciousness that the evolutionary process not only produced increasingly complex organisms, but that their awareness became increasingly acute too. Now this wasn't just for human beings but for all organisms, demonstrating, as he hoped to, that all things respond to the stimuli of other things, and that through evolution this sensitising of the ecology of the natural world was increased as organisms became more complex.

Today there is a good deal of interest in behaviour in the study of all forms of life, from viruses mutating to create new forms, as we saw, for example, during the COVID-19 pandemic, in the need for pharmaceutical companies to create new vaccines, and tweak them once a fresh strain of a virus appeared, through the reach of fungi mycelium within ancient woodland, the spread of which is quite staggering in its extent and general infiltration, better known is the capacity for bees and ants to communicate and rebuild after damage to their colonies, and, ultimately, we observe too the higher animals and plants responding to climate change and the encroachment of humanity.

It is the thought of what progress demands of human society today that confounds us with the complexity of the issues, from concerns about

[55] Christopher F. Mooney, *Teilhard de Chardin and the Mystery of Christ*, p. 22.

personal and national security to the invasive screening of individuals, especially when crossing barriers from one jurisdiction to another, that is justified by the need to keep everyone safe. Individuals act, 'in the knowledge that the choice [they make] will have its repercussions through countless centuries and upon countless human beings.'[56] Words that could have appeared in a journal or newspaper today.

One of the things that concentrates the minds of all thinking people in the twenty-first century is the major issue of dealing with the effects of climate change, avoiding misuse of the Earth's finite resources, curbing pollution and restoring damaged environments, preventing war and establishing peace in conflict zones. There is a:

> *[...] profound need for unity which pervades the world and crowning it with renewed faith in Christ the Physical Centre of Creation; finding in this need the natural energy required for the renewal of the world's life.*[57]

The crying desire for unity of purpose in action, and willingness to promote investment, as a primary resource and concern in the environment, is one that will be heard in every country and from all peoples. However, greed and a selfish attitude from those with the wealth and power to cope with the effects of climate change, and whose lack of concern for anything from dying corals to polluted rivers, to famine in regions becoming deserts to those whose lives and livelihoods are

---

[56] Teilhard de Chardin, *The Future of Man*, p. 18.
[57] Teilhard de Chardin, *The Future of Man*, p. 23.

swept away by wildfires or floods, will mean that little or nothing happens unless it comes knocking at their door, so targets are abandoned and opportunities lost. Yet, as the writer to the Colossians says, all things are ultimately subject to the divine influence. They always have been and they always will be. The power is invisible and the action not seen, but Christ is the one to bring order to human failure, to bring down the mighty and raise up the meek of the earth. In the face of everything that appears to contradict this very fact, let us pray that our Lord will restore and renew the hearts that are broken and hopes dashed in the rush for short-term gain, and that the aggression that brings misery to millions upon millions of human lives may be thwarted by the international will to create a just world order.

PRAYER

Father,
in the power of the Holy Spirit
may the life of your Son bring the world to
    its senses,
with love may we serve our neighbour,
and show the world that we believe
that Christ is the Light of the World,
and, as such, the inspiration
for all that we do that is good and life
    enhancing,
in him who is the firstborn of all Creation,
the same, your Son, Jesus Christ.
Amen.

DAY 28 (28th September)

Christ – Active, Incarnate, Life-giving

Philippians 2:4

UNITY IS NOT some theoretical estate that Christians believe in and hold dear because they imagine that it is praiseworthy and good. It does not reside simply in mutual interests and actions and the sharing of the product of human thought, but rather it exists in the inner recesses of our being, and, whilst we may observe physical progress through dialogue and formal agreements, the Christian will wish to go deeper and understand how the Incarnate Christ is related to this striving for unity, in fact he is its author, and understand how faith is vital to the very process of finding that we are one. Pierre Teilhard's view is illustrated by Christopher Mooney through Karl Rahner, thus:

Man cannot fulfil his spiritual or indeed his supernatural life without embodying this fulfilment in material reality; without a turning towards the world, an infusing of the spiritual into the material.

> *Hence the world is really a unity, one thing. The actual interdependence of one thing upon everything else corresponds to the original creative will of God, and objectifies itself in the fundamental mutual relationship based on the essence of individual things themselves.*[58]

This surely is the essence of the proclamation of a Creation Season, that all our appreciation of the World, whether in its beauty and mystery and wonder, or in humanity's disregard for these very things and treatment of it as a utilitarian source of its existence, leading to the current crisis of management of the Earth's resources, comes down to these facts: The Incarnate Christ is bound up in God's Creation and Redemption; his worship is essentially inseparable from life on Earth; our health and the health of the planet are of everlasting concern to him, and should be to us all who inhabit this amazing place in the Universe.

> *Let each of you look not only to his own interests, but also to the interests of others.*

Can we indeed do anything other than what Paul bids the Philippians to undertake? We may read this as between an individual and a neighbour, such as occurred in the Parable of the Good Samaritan, but thinking much wider, cosmically even, the interests of present and future generations combine with reflections on what has gone and imagination of what may yet occur. We

[58]   Christopher F. Mooney, *Teilhard de Chardin and the Mystery of Christ* (Collins, 1966), p. 102.

'cannot fulfil his spiritual or indeed his supernatural life without embodying this fulfilment in material reality; without a turning towards the world, an infusing of the spiritual into the material'. No, indeed, and if this Season is turning our thoughts to what we should dwell on and away from self-centred concerns, important though they may be, then this period, from the beginning of September to the feast day of St Francis of Assisi, is declared hopefully and positively in the fullness of its vital importance.

PRAYER

Heavenly Father,
grant us grace we pray,
to seek in humility the deep truth
that Christ your Incarnate Son,
through his very nature,
holds all created things in unity,
and that we in harmony with nature
share our lives with all life on Earth,
created and redeemed in love,
inspiring love within us for all others.
In Jesus' name we pray.
Amen.

DAY 29 (29th September)

Michaelmas

Tobit 12:15-18, 22

> *'I am Raphael, one of the seven angels who stand ready and enter before the glory of the Lord.'*
>
> *The two of them were shaken and threw themselves face down, for they were afraid. But he said to them, 'Do not be afraid; peace be with you. Bless God forevermore. As for me, when I was with you, I was not acting on my own will but by the will of God. Bless him each and every day; sing his praises [...]' They kept blessing God and singing his praises, and they acknowledged God for these marvellous deeds of his, that an angel of God had appeared to them.*

MICHAELMAS, OR THE festival of St Michael and All Angels, is one that, in the nature of things, rarely falls on a Sunday, which is a pity as it is one of the most special days in the Christian Calendar. This morning the lectionary may direct that we read from the Book of Tobit (Tobit 12:6-end), part of the Apocrypha, and the account of a man of piety and charitable mindset, who nevertheless found himself poor and blind. The book also introduces a woman Sarah, who lived far away. She suffered from demon possession.

The story comes to a lovely ending when both are healed, and Tobias, Tobit's son marries Sarah. Tobit speaks of losing his sight when he was fifty-eight and regaining it eight years later. The agent of God's healing was the archangel Raphael.

Raphael reveals himself as one of seven holy angels, but we know, by name, of only four archangels: Michael and Gabriel from the New Testament, Raphael and Uriel from the Apocrypha. St Anne's Cathedral in Belfast, where I served as dean, has the four archangels carved high up, one in each corner of the nave, as with other much more ancient Romanesque churches. I often felt a sense of them looking down upon us, and I imagine that the practice of carving them in this position was out of a sense of angelic protection for the congregation.

Raphael is the archangel linked to healing. Hence the Guild of St Raphael, and other such references. Gabriel we think of from the Christmas stories, and Michael is the one who leads the angelic armies of God; Uriel is depicted as holding the orb of the sun and is said to be the most clear sighted, but he was the angel who, in Milton's *Paradise Lost*, is deceived by Satan's wily talk and allows him to slip through to disturb the paradise of Eden.

Once, visiting the village of Mortehoe on the north Devon coast, I found the church open on a day during the week. It is a lovely ancient building (dedicated to St Mary, not, in fact, to St Michael and All Angels) with some very interesting features including a window of the four archangels. Out of all of the stained-glass windows, this one glowed in the August sunshine, with the 1905 angelic mosaics on the walls nearby, both designed by Selwyn Image,

Slade Professor of Art at Oxford,[59] adding to the effect. The church must feel to its worshippers as filled with light and the presence of the angels, the messengers of God, whose place in the Scriptures may seem to us today somewhat strange, but remind us just how often their presence is key to a message from God being delivered to his people.

On this Michaelmas Day, such thoughts as we may have of the angelic messengers and their place in our own life stories, the critical place of important proclamation being received is good to hear, for without doubt the knowledge we possess of the state of Nature, and the environmental catastrophe that is being experienced by many in the world of the 2020s, comes to us with the force of an archangel's voice and the stamp of the Creator's authority.

Yet the messengers of God are rarely archangels, more often ordinary mortals, who happen to say the right thing at the right moment for us, and frequently unconsciously. When Simone Weil was searching for the meaning of divine love and dwelling on the Passion of Christ, she had this experience:

> *There was a young English Catholic there from whom I gained my first idea of the supernatural power of the Sacraments because of the truly angelic radiance with which he seemed to be clothed after going to Communion. Chance – for I always prefer saying chance rather than Providence – made him a messenger to me. For he told me of the existence of those English poets of the XVIIth century who are named*

[59] Referenced from Simon Jenkins, *England's Thousand Best Churches* (Penguin Books, 1999), p. 134.

metaphysical. In reading them later on, I discovered the poem […] It is called 'Love'. I learned it by heart.

Often, at the culminating point of a violent headache, I make myself say it over, concentrating all my attention upon it and clinging with all my soul to the tenderness it enshrines. I used to think I was merely reciting a beautiful poem, but without my knowing it the recitation had the virtue of a prayer. It was during one of these recitations that […] Christ himself came down and took possession of me.[60]

The cause of our inspiration may or may not be linked to the Creation which holds our devotional attention during these days, but we may be assured that however the vision of the future lies within us, its presence is not a chance encounter with truth, but a pointer towards something deeper and requiring thought and possibly action. In Simone Weil's experience it led her to pray, which in itself was a revelation to her.

PRAYER

Father
in Love we seek to meet
and greet the ones we love and long for,
whilst serving all, and learning the ways
of all who share human life and find
mercy and forgiveness in you
and your Son, Jesus Christ.
Amen.

[60] Simone Weil, *Waiting on God*, pp. 20, 21. The reference is to George Herbert's poem, 'Love (III)'.

DAY 30 (30th September)

Exploitation

James 5:4

THE EXPLOITATION OF many peoples in the world today is one of the great scandals of human existence, and often linked to environmental damage as well. In the Letter of James the example given is one of slave labour in the fields, but many comparable expressions of exploitation, people trafficking, stealing resources, the forcible moving of population, and damage to land, forests and buildings, has resulted in misery and untold and incalculable moral debt that the rich and powerful owe to the poor of the world. Some of these events are historic, perhaps from long ago, and, in those cases, the seeking of restitution is a burning issue, and not easily settled. Having spent much of his scientific investigation delving into the past, through palaeontology and geology, Teilhard wrote the following in a letter in September 1935:

It is almost as though, for reasons arising from the progress of my own science, the past and its discovery had ceased to interest me. The past has revealed to me how the future is built and preoccupation with the future tends to sweep everything else aside. It is precisely that I may be able to speak with authority about the future that it is essential for me to establish myself more firmly than before as a specialist on the past.[61]

Teilhard de Chardin was writing in relation to his evolutionary theory, but the parallel is there, as he saw aspects other than the purely physical adapting over the course of evolutionary history. In terms of human exploitation, and crimes against humanity in general, there appeared to have been progress in the wake of the Second World War especially, with international agreements sought and curbs on weapons, the establishment of the United Nations, etc. However, lessons learnt through the World Wars of the twentieth century have been eroded by a new generation of aggressive and repressive regimes that at the time of writing appear to have little diplomatic restraint, in fact diplomacy when entered into is used as a period to pause, regroup and rearm for further conflict, inflicting unimaginable suffering, stirring hatred, and causing incalculable environmental damage.

In the French original, and copied through into the English translation, the editor of the travel letters of Teilhard de Chardin placed the words '*The past has revealed to me how the future is built*' in italics, with the comment that they

[61]   Teilhard de Chardin, *Letters from a Traveller,* 1962, p. 160.

'are a cardinal expression'[62] of his thought. The Creation Season provides just that sort of historical perspective back to the earliest days, to demonstrate that what we are experiencing today is not unexpected. The question that humanity will face and answer in the coming decade is whether or not the revelation of the past can sufficiently restrain the trends to war, and growing power politics over how potential flash points such as the Arctic, the eastern edge of NATO, and the South China Sea can be managed for the good of all people and the preservation of the planet.

If protectionism and economic power, with little attention to aid for the poor and disadvantaged, aggravating the state of injustice that already exists, is to be the cause of the unravelling of the current period of international diplomacy, let us hope and pray that the ultimate outcome will involve compassion and support for those in extreme need leading to a rebuilding and restitution on the scale of the post-Second World War period. The letter of James has given us the heading for thought, of labourers who mow a farmer's field and are not paid, but in reality there are many ways in which such exploitation manifests itself and is managed, and the cost to the individual is, as ever, immense.

[62] Teilhard de Chardin, *Letters from a Traveller,* 1962, p. 160.

PRAYER

In sorrow for past misdeeds
we make our prayer to you, Lord,
acknowledging how our acts may not
have reflected the highest ideals of our lives,
and someone, somewhere, has suffered.
Grant us the grace and the sense
to use our time and effort to create
a world that is just and fair for all.
May love be our aim
and compassion the mark of our lives
in Christ we pray.
Amen.

DAY 31 (1st October)

Learning the Lessons

2 Timothy 2:2

NOSTALGIA IS A powerful emotion that can incline us to backward-looking and seeing that sight through rose-tinted spectacles, but there are things of the past that can and should resonate in such a way that gems of truth and hard-won lessons from history are not lost. Oral tradition is as vital as the written record, for it holds the perspective of those who pass on the message. One day in 2020 I visited Brownsea Island in Poole harbour and jotted down the following:

From the moment that one steps away from Church Field, the clatter of the boat and the chatter of the other visitors falls into the background, and becomes a wallpaper on which is imprinted the bustle of Poole harbour, the castle, the NT welcome, the signage and the way markers and you simply emerge from it and leave it where it is. The Church on the rise, the peacocks strutting on the browned grass, the shadow of heavy oaks and the dusty well-worn paths. All of that becomes two-dimensional and static. It'll wait, for three hours and more, as the years slip away and the child in you sees possibilities in every hole and sparkle, oddly-formed branch or coloured stone. Eyes beyond even them draw you deeper into the mystery of this place; this isle of adventure; this place where no jet-ski should be heard, or jarring command – and no limit be set on the imagining.

Walking clockwise, and travelling westward, the path is soon amongst the trees; ancient pines and noble oaks; red squirrels scamper and bees hum and crickets set up a cracking racket. The heat is rising from the baked ground and light is glinting through the straight trunks that draw your eye to the blue sea below and beyond. It is dusty and stony – just as it should be. This is not an island for wet meadows and dripping moss; this is a place of burning possibility in a summer made for holidays and endless hours lost in wild escape and unworried happiness.

Don't speak. Just close your eyes and wonder. That root is not a root, it is the carefully placed marker directing us through the thicket of pines that holds secrets in the deep recesses of their cracked and venerable bark. This is a place alive with surprises that flutter or burst into view, but all the time it is not what is there, it is what it arouses, that holds the timeless amnesia, and makes for childhood dreams and visions of old men, that meet somewhere between a twirling seed caught in the sunlight and a stone bounced on a glittering sea.

How many boys have lifted that stone at camp, or girls climbed those inviting branches, lain across those camping fields or torn through bracken in the heat of chase. Laughter hangs in the air, but is not there and childhood screams of fun ripple across the silent flowing seed-heads. A scraped knee and banged head are somehow lost in the games and campfires and shouts of discovery; memories that seem to take root and grow, with the breath of the wind and the smell of the pines.

This is no place to mope, for, even under the dark hanging branches in the deeper shade, the poignancy of what is lost in adulthood refuels the imagination with hope, and counters evil thoughts with the indestructible; the loving; the joyful; the need to know that goodness and compassion will, with love, patience, gentleness, long-suffering and hope, find their resting place in your heart and with them the source of all created things, the God of truth, mercy and peace; ever reforming and restoring in Christ, forsaken and risen, offering his life that all may share in what is forever new.

As this Season of Creation draws to its close, we have a few things to contemplate that go beyond the present day. We turn tomorrow to Revelation and the New Heaven and the New Earth, but as we think about how we act, and where to place our resources in this mortal existence, there is a deep and lasting treasure to be recalled. This Creation is God's, now ours, and we are stewards of a beautiful and complex planet, and the responsibility for it has been handed to us from former generations that have made mistakes, but have valued its wonders too, and we shall hand it on to the generations yet to come, whose love of their Earth home will be as ours. In remembering what is not just of practical necessity for physical life, but of spiritual and emotional power in Nature, we may gain a greater sense of urgency in maintaining, and enhancing, the life that we experience. Can humanity, even at this late stage in the attempt to heal the damage to our planet, seek the miracle of peace through the miracle of dialogue, and work co-operatively for the good of every living thing on Earth? Let us hope so, and resolve from this moment to be part of the source of that miracle.

Teilhard de Chardin expresses a spiritual awakening in these words:

> *A breeze passes in the night. When did it spring up? Whence does it come? Whither is it going? No man knows. No one can compel the spirit, the gaze or the light of God to descend upon him.*
>
> *On some given day a man suddenly becomes conscious that he is alive to a particular perception of the divine spread everywhere about him. Question him. When did this state begin for him? He cannot tell. All he knows is that a new spirit has crossed his life.*[63]

PRAYER

Father,
may the blessing of passing things
recall us to those of eternity,
as a brief encounter may lead
us to love that for which we had not known,
but now do, through the Holy Spirit's
inspiration, transformation and new life
in Christ Jesus our Lord.
Amen.

[63]   Teilhard de Chardin, *Le Milieu Divin*, pp. 128, 129.

DAY 32 (2nd October)

The New Heaven and the New Earth

Revelation 21:1-7

Then I saw a new heaven and a new earth; for the first heaven and the first earth had passed away, and the sea was no more. And I saw the holy city, the new Jerusalem, coming down out of heaven from God, prepared as a bride adorned for her husband. And I heard a loud voice from the throne saying,

'See, the home of God is among mortals.
He will dwell with them;
they will be his peoples,
and God himself will be with them;
he will wipe every tear from their eyes.
Death will be no more;
mourning and crying and pain will be no more,
for the first things have passed away.'

And the one who was seated on the throne said, 'See, I am making all things new.' Also he said, 'Write this, for these words are trustworthy and true.' Then he said to me, 'It is done! I am the Alpha and the Omega, the beginning and the end. To the thirsty I will give water as a gift from the spring of the water of life. Those who conquer will inherit these things, and I will be their God and they will be my children.'

THE TEXT FOR today assumes the consummation of all things, as St John the Divine sees it in the vision of the New Heaven and the New Earth. The hope is there that the distress that is the experience for so many will be ended for ever, and the family of God will be complete and at peace.

Teilhard de Chardin questioned our readiness to receive this state of affairs and our lack of expectation that such a transformation will happen:

> *No doubt [...] our prayers and actions are conscientiously directed to bringing about 'the coming of God's kingdom'. But in fact how many of us are genuinely moved in the depths of our hearts by the wild hope that our earth will be recast? Who is there who sets a course in the midst of our darkness towards the first glimmer of a real dawn? Where is the Christian in whom the impatient longing for Christ succeeds, not in submerging (as it should) the cares of human love and human interests, but even in counter-balancing them? [...] We persist in saying that we keep vigil in expectation of the Master. But in reality we should have to admit, if we were sincere, that we no longer expect anything.* [64]

The Church is much engaged with the issues of our day and has been under the spotlight for its serious failings in recent years. The emphasis on putting its own house in order, especially in the Western World, has been of such essential engagement with the immediate present and

[64] Teilhard de Chardin, *Le Milieu Divin*, p. 152.

past, that even the glimmer of expectation for the future that might have resided in the intention of looking further and deeper, as we are drawn that way by Christ, has largely been lost in the practicalities of more contemporary challenges. The Church in our generation may not be the most spiritually aware in its history, and as we look to St John's vision, we know also that the popular genre of books and films of fantasy to some extent erodes our hold on reality, as Christians attempt to envision eternity and heavenly life from the ancient texts of Scripture. Teilhard's words, 'in reality we should have to admit, if we were sincere, *that we no longer expect anything*' have a chilling feel about them, and certainly, a challenge.

However, the vision of John is there for us, and the hope which it expresses is in harmony with our deepest desires. When these verses from Revelation chapter 21 are read in Church, or elsewhere, they read as a prophecy, and to some extent an indictment on humanity's woes. They recall how low we have sunk from the idea of a loving God whose Creation, of which we are a part, is groaning under the immeasurable force of our destructive tendencies. Yet, John's vision reminds us, that beyond all things, God has a plan which is unaffected by our failure, residing as it does in the incarnate life of Christ, in whom and through whom all things shall continue to exist, and be renewed for eternity. It is recognisably a place that we can relate to, however, for in John's vision of Earth and Heaven there is a city, a dwelling place, and one which has features of which we are familiar. It may be radically different in the sense that it is renewed in ways that make it perfect, but the character of the original Creation remains; it is not an entirely alien new home.

From the perspective of the Creation Season this is helpful and instructive, for the dangers that humanity run have a finite course, and the fact that there is an ultimate new place, actually gives the impetus to redouble efforts to maintain the physical world as we know it – in as near a state of perfection as we can make it – and have received it. But, the scene does look into eternity, and with the perception that it is marked by an end to suffering and death for ever.

PRAYER

Heavenly Father
we look to the vision of John
as you revealed eternity to him,
and rest in the knowledge of what he saw.
With this resting on our hearts and minds,
bring us to that place of action in this world
where suffering and death are still real,
and from where we draw close
to those who need what we have to offer,
and bring healing to your damaged world,
in Jesus Christ our Lord.
Amen.

DAY 33 (3rd October)

The Healing of the Nations

Revelation 22:1, 2

> *Then the angel showed me the river of the water of life, bright as crystal, flowing from the throne of God and of the Lamb through the middle of the street of the city. On either side of the river is the tree of life with its twelve kinds of fruit, producing its fruit each month; and the leaves of the tree are for the healing of the nations.*

THROUGHOUT THE BOOK of Revelation there are references to other parts of the Scriptures. In the case of the water of life we are taken back to Joel,[65] Ezekiel[66] and Zechariah,[67] covering the period before, during and after the Exile. Here now at the end of time the river appears in all its refreshing and fruitful life, flowing from the throne. This text is linked to the flow of water divinely channelled that appears throughout the Bible, from the early chapters of Genesis to this point; this new beginning, recapitulating Genesis, as we read yesterday: *'See, I am making all things new'*.

[65] Joel 3:18.
[66] Ezekiel 47:1-9.
[67] Zechariah 14:8.

Who can fail to perceive the great symbolic gesture of baptism in this general history of matter? Christ immerses himself in the waters of Jordan, symbol of the forces of the earth. These he sanctifies. And as he emerges, in the words of St Gregory of Nyssa, with the water which runs off his body he elevates the whole world.

Immersion and emergence; participation in things and sublimation; possession and renunciation; crossing through and being borne onwards – that is the twofold yet single movement which answers the challenge of matter in order to save it.

Matter, you in whom I find both seduction and strength, you in whom I find blandishment and virility, you who can enrich and destroy, I surrender myself to your mighty layers, with faith in the heavenly influences which have sweetened and purified your waters. *The virtue of Christ has passed into you.* Let your attractions lead me forward, let your sap be the food that nourishes me; let your resistance give me toughness; let your robberies and inroads give me freedom. And finally let your whole being lead me towards Godhead.[68]

The healing power of nature has long been recognised, and I recall well, in a part of my life, finding my garden to be of immense help whilst coming to terms with change that had caused significant loss. Gardens with water have inspired the naturalist as much as the poet and musician; flowing water calms the senses

---

[68]   Teilhard de Chardin, *Le Milieu Divin*, pp. 110, 111.

and soothes the spirit. However, the Garden of Eden has been transformed into the City with its streets and trees. This could be perceived as a 'garden city' indeed, with its trees bearing fruit and its leaves for healing. However we may imagine it, the water flows through it and onwards, refreshing and bringing life. Without the water, there would be no fruit, no leaves and consequently no healing.

Psalm 42 reminds us of something further, of the need of water to drink, and the thirst for what is yet deeper, for God in our hearts, for it is in this psalm that desire is expressed as the thirst of a deer: 'Like the deer that yearns for longing streams, so my soul is yearning for you, my God.'

This is a psalm which expresses feelings of exile, and engages us with the desire to be where we should be; where tears are gone and feelings of separation and dislocation are changed to the sound of rejoicing and thanksgiving, such as we read yesterday from Revelation 21. Psalm 42 is indeed a powerful psalm; one that breaks into the heart of the one who is crying in anguish, and with it asking the question of which the answer is abundantly obvious, 'Why are you cast down, O my soul?'

The writer feels mocked and taunted. His way back to some semblance of sense, some balance of emotional stability, is found by using his memory. This forms a bridge for him to travel over, but then to return. His recall of things out of exile is not driving him deeper into despair, it is bringing to mind just how much God is central to his life; how much the reality of God's presence is in every aspect of his being. As he thinks and thinks of how things have been, he comes to see the divine presence even in the situation that he does not like, but is now better equipped in which to live.

This beautiful psalm has a lesson for those brought low for any reason, but may suit the mood that could well be catching in our day: a need that suggests that the current crisis can only go on and on. It may change a bit, but the place that has been emotionally and spiritually found is one of inescapable exile. I can understand that feeling. There may be minor ups and downs, but the basic situation is of a cast-down spirit. This psalm is the tonic for anyone veering down that particular rabbit-hole, because this writer has been there before us. It is not a psalm reflecting someone snapping out of a depressed state, it is the record of someone on a journey from sadness to hope, and reaching for the path as a thirsty deer glimpses the running waters of a stream. So may the journey begin today; may we walk it prayerfully together; may we know the refreshing stream to which we travel; and may we find the place of the living God, where he still is, in the depth of our hearts.

PRAYER

Creator God,
As we look towards the world
in all its beauty,
let us dwell on the water,
that brings life, but may drown it too.

Thirsting, we seek your face
and look towards the hope that is ours,
while strength and life endure,
and Christ is all in all
before us, behind us and within us
always and forever.
Amen.

DAY 34 (4th October)

St Francis of Assisi's Day
Matthew 11:25-30

> *At that time Jesus said, 'I thank you, Father, Lord of heaven and earth, because you have hidden these things from the wise and the intelligent and have revealed them to infants; yes, Father, for such was your gracious will. All things have been handed over to me by my Father; and no one knows the Son except the Father, and no one knows the Father except the Son and anyone to whom the Son chooses to reveal him. 'Come to me, all you that are weary and are carrying heavy burdens, and I will give you rest. Take my yoke upon you, and learn from me; for I am gentle and humble in heart, and you will find rest for your souls. For my yoke is easy, and my burden is light.'*

MANY PEOPLE OVER the centuries have been inspired by St Francis of Assisi, seeing in him someone as close to the person of Christ as it is possible to be: selfless, childlike in the simplicity of love's demands, open and fearless in the face of those whose faith and love is compromised by caveats, yet have the power and wealth to make a difference to their neighbour but do not. It is not surprising that Simone Weil was drawn to

Francis, not out of admiration cultivated from afar, but by being driven to believe that if she could be of any use to anyone it could only be along the same path that Francis trod.

> *As for the spirit of poverty, I do not remember any moment when it was not in me, although only to that unhappily small extent which is compatible with my imperfection. I fell in love with Saint Francis of Assisi as soon as I came to know about him. I always believed and hoped that one day Fate would force upon me the condition of a vagabond and a beggar which he embraced freely. Actually I felt the same way about prison.*[69]

In finishing the Season of Creation on St Francis of Assisi's Day that fact that he was so close to the natural world, and is said to have preached to the birds and the animals, is easy to understand. The contemplation of him bearing with the injury and suffering of the created world in all its fullness is perhaps even closer to the point. The material condition of those who had, and have, nothing but what they stand up in is a state close to the condition in which the world as an environmental entity is closely related. Sites that once were ecologically rich and varied have been stripped bare of their diverse character and may have become even, effectively, new deserts, poisoned swamps, polluted and almost lifeless, except for the few organisms that can survive under the most extreme conditions. Francis's love of all living things is one which it is easier to recapture than his embracing of the poverty

[69] Simone Weil, *Waiting on God*, p. 18.

and humility that is transforming in its gift to humankind and to Creation in its totality.

Simone Weil found the place of Assisi of immense significance, but ultimately the destination was the cross; there, indeed, all that this Creation Season calls for is met by the redemptive act of Christ. At that point and in that moment we find the place from which to rise to take up our place as advocates of the call to healing, that is the cry of every damaged fragment of God's wonderful work in the Creation of this beautiful world which is our home:

In 1937 I had two marvellous days at Assisi. There, alone in the little XIIth Century Romanesque chapel of Santa Maria degli Angeli, an incomparable marvel of purity where Saint Francis often used to pray, something stronger than I was compelled me for the first time in my life to go down on my knees.

In 1938 I spent ten days at Solesmes, from Palm Sunday to Easter Tuesday, following all the liturgical services. I was suffering from splitting headaches; each sound hurt me like a blow; by an extreme effort of concentration I was able to rise above this wretched flesh, to leave it to suffer by itself, heaped up in a corner, and to find a pure and perfect joy in the unimaginable beauty of the chanting and the words. This experience enabled me by analogy to get a better understanding of the possibility of loving divine love in the midst of affliction. It goes without saying that in the course of these services the thought of the Passion of Christ entered my being once and for all.[70]

[70] Simone Weil, *Waiting on God,* p. 20.

So the Season of Creation ends for another year at the foot of the cross; the meeting place for lovers of Christ; the learning place for lovers of the world. In joy we look to the beauty that surrounds us, and in penitence and faith commit ourselves to a closer fellowship with each other and to all God's creatures. May the divine blessing that continues to gift this life so bounteously carry us onward to the holy city, where the light of Christ bathes all perpetually and where the scars we bear, with and for each other, are eternally healed.

THE PRAYER OF SAINT FRANCIS

Lord, make me an instrument of your peace.
Where there is hatred, let me bring love.
Where there is offence, let me bring pardon.
Where there is discord, let me bring union.
Where there is error, let me bring truth.
Where there is doubt, let me bring faith.
Where there is despair, let me bring hope.
Where there is darkness, let me bring your
    light.
Where there is sadness, let me bring joy.
O Lord, grant that I may not so much seek
to be consoled as to console,
to be understood as to understand,
to be loved as to love,
for it is in giving that one receives,
it is in self-forgetting that one finds,
it is in forgiving that one is forgiven,
it is in dying that one awakens to eternal life.